RANGE, TRANSPOSITION & TUNING

A GUIDE FOR OVER
500
MUSICAL INSTRUMENTS

COMPILED AND EDITED BY

ROBERT G. BORNSTEIN

Library of Congress Catolog Card Number: 64-22747

ISBN 1-4950-2265-X

7777 W. BLUEMOUND RD. P.O. BOX 13819 MILWAUKEE, WI 53213

Visit Hal Leonard Online at
www.halleonard.com

CONTENTS

EXPLANATION OF USE

For **WOODWIND, BRASS, KEYBOARDS, and PERCUSSION INSTRUMENTS**, the semibreve-notes (o) (otherwise known as whole notes) show the *practical range* of the instrument in actual sounds. The notes shown in crotchet heads (●) (otherwise known as quarter notes) are extreme notes which represent the following:

- Notes playable by the use of specially adjusted instruments.
- Notes playable according to the ability of individual performers.
- Possible but impractical playing notes.

The extreme notes shown are practical extremes only. Most professional performers, particularly brass, can exceed that which is considered practical or even extreme.

For **STRING INSTRUMENTS,** the crotchet heads (●) (quarter notes) indicate the open notes tuning in concert key.

The square note (■) shows the note that is written to sound middle C. The sole purpose of this note is to show the transposition of the instrument, (if any), and *in no way is this note related to the instrument's playing range.*

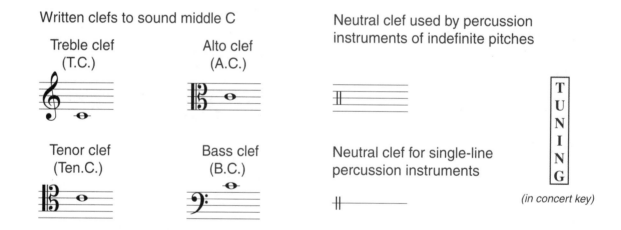

Written clefs to sound middle C

Treble clef (T.C.)   Alto clef (A.C.)

Tenor clef (Ten.C.)   Bass clef (B.C.)

Neutral clef used by percussion instruments of indefinite pitches

Neutral clef for single-line percussion instruments

TUNING

(in concert key)

EXAMPLES

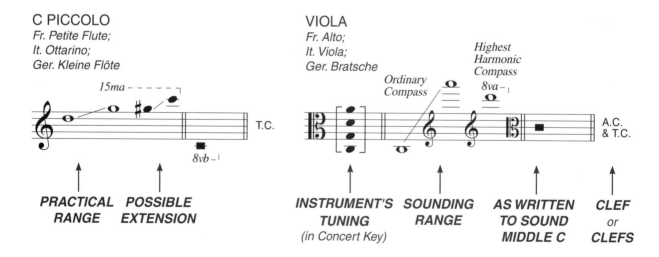

C PICCOLO
Fr. Petite Flute;
It. Ottarino;
Ger. Kleine Flöte

15ma - - - - -

8vb -

T.C.

PRACTICAL RANGE   **POSSIBLE EXTENSION**

VIOLA
Fr. Alto;
It. Viola;
Ger. Bratsche

Ordinary Compass   *Highest Harmonic Compass*   *8va -*

A.C. & T.C.

INSTRUMENT'S TUNING
(in Concert Key)   **SOUNDING RANGE**   **AS WRITTEN TO SOUND MIDDLE C**   **CLEF** *or* **CLEFS**

THE PLAYING RANGE

There are numerous Luthiers in the world of string instruments. They are talented craftsmen who manufacture customized as well as standard string instruments. Therefore, the playing range of some instruments may differ from the standard range, depending on the manufacturer as well as the ability of the performer.

THE TUNINGS

It is a common practice of performers of string instruments to use their own tunings as well as the common tunings that are notated in this book. The bar lines divide the string courses.

THE PLAYING CLEFS

Players of string instruments are usually capable of reading more than one clef. In fact, it is possible that two or more players of the same instrument may each select different clefs. For example, each member of a group of Mandolin players may select a different clef to read for the same piece of music.

THE TRANSPOSITION

Transpositions are shown by the indication of which note is played to sound middle C on the piano. Please note that Turkish instruments are usually transposed a fourth higher.

_____

ACKNOWLEDGEMENTS

Many thanks and appreciation to all the musical instrument manufacturers and professional musicians from around the world, for furnishing the information in this book.

I hope that this will be a valuable reference for music students and composers.

Robert G. Bornstein

PICCOLOS - FLUTES
FIFE

Db PICCOLO
Fr. Petite Flûte en Reb;
It. Ottavino in Reb;
Ger. Kleine Flöte in Des

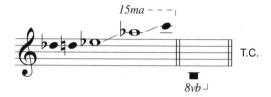

T.C.

C FLUTE
Fr. Flûte;
It. Flauto;
Ger. Flöte

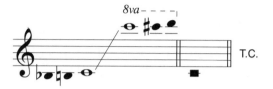

T.C.

C PICCOLO
Fr. Petite Flûte;
It. Ottavino;
Ger. Kleine Flöte

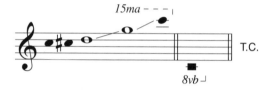

T.C.

FLAGEOLET (in G)
Fr. Clarinette en La;
It. Clarinetto in La;
Ger. Klarinette in A

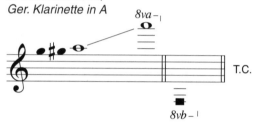

T.C.

Eb SOPRANO FLUTE
Fr. Flûte Dessus en Mib;
It. Flauto Soprano in Mib;
Ger. Sopranflöte in Es

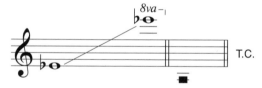

T.C.

G ALTO FLUTE
Fr. Flûte Alto;
It. Flautone;
Ger. Altflöte

T.C.

BASS FLUTE (in C)
Fr. Flûte Basse;
It. Flauto Basso;
Ger. Bassflöte

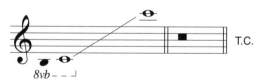

T.C.

FIFE (in Bb - 6 hole)
Fr. Fifre;
It. Piffero;
Ger. Querpfeife

T.C.

(The Keyed Fife in Bb can play the same range *chromatically*.)

DOUBLE REEDS

SOPRANO OBOE in E♭
Fr. Hautbois Dessus en Mi♭;
It. Soprano Oboe in Mi♭;
Ger. Sopran Oboe in Es

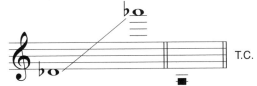

T.C.

HECKELPHON

T.C.

OBOE
Fr. Hautbois;
It. Oboe;
Ger. Oboe

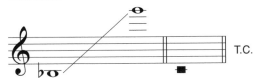

T.C.

BARITONE OBOE (in C)
Fr. Hautbois Bariton;
It. Oboe Baritono;
Ger. Bariton Oboe

T.C.

OBOE d'AMORE (in A)
Fr. Hautbois d'Amour

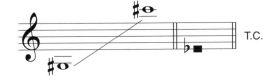

T.C.

MUSETTE (Keyless Oboe)

T.C.

ENGLISH HORN (in F)
Fr. Cor Anglais;
It. Corno Inglese;
Ger. Englisches Horn

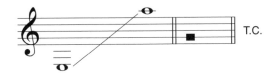

T.C.

BASSOON
Fr. Basson;
It. Fagotto;
Ger. Fagott

B.C.
T.C.
&
Ten.C.

CONTRA BASSOON
Fr. Contrebasson;
It. Contrafagotto;
Ger. Kontrafagott

B.C.

SARRUSOPHONES

These are double-reed, metal instruments that have the key-mechanism of the saxophone. They were invented in 1856 by the French bandmaster Sarrus, who wanted an additional complete section of voices in French bands. These double-reed instruments have the tone quality of Oboes, English Horns and Bassoons, and can be played with single-reed mouthpieces. However, when single-reed mouthpieces are used, the tenors, altos and sopranos lose a little of their richness and English Horn quality.

B♭ SOPRANO SARRUSOPHONE
Fr. Sarrusophone Dessus en Si♭;
It. Sarrusofone Soprano in Si♭;
Ger. Sopran Sarrusophone in B

E♭ BARITONE SARRUSOPHONE
Fr. Sarrusophone Bariton en Mi♭;
It. Sarrusofone Baritono in Mi♭;
Ger. Bariton Sarrusophone in Es

E♭ CONTRALTO SARRUSOPHONE
Fr. Sarrusophone Contralto en Mi♭;
It. Sarrusofone Contralto in Mi♭;
Ger. Contralt Sarrusophone in Es

B♭ BASS SARRUSOPHONE
Fr. Sarrusophone Basse en Si♭;
It. Sarrusofone Basso in Si♭;
Ger. Bass Sarrusophone in B

B♭ TENOR SARRUSOPHONE
Fr. Sarrusophone Tenor en Si♭;
It. Sarrusofone Tenore in Si♭;
Ger. Tenor Sarrusophone in B

E♭ CONTRA BASS SARRUSOPHONE
Fr. Sarrusophone Contrebasse en Mi♭;
It. Sarrusofone Contrabasso in Mi♭;
Ger. Kontrabass Sarrusophone in Es

C CONTRA BASS SARRUSOPHONE
Fr. Sarrusophone Contrebasse en Ut;
It. Sarrusofone Contrabass in Do;
Ger. Kontrabass Sarrusophone in C

CLARINETS

Eb CLARINET
Fr. Petite Clarinette en Mib;
It. Clarinetto Piccolo in Mib;
Ger. Klarinette in Es

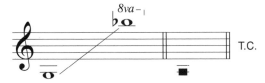

Bb CLARINET
Fr. Clarinette en Sib;
It. Clarinetto in Sib;
Ger. Klarinette in B

D CLARINET
Fr. Clarinette en Re;
It. Clarinetto in Re;
Ger. Klarinette in D

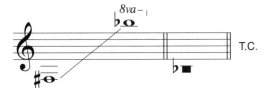

A CLARINET
Fr. Clarinette en La;
It. Clarinetto in La;
Ger. Klarinette in A

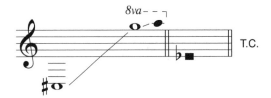

C CLARINET
Fr. Clarinette on Ut;
It. Clarinetto in Do;
Ger. Klarinette in C

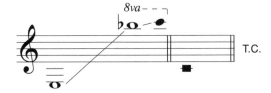

Bb HECKELCLARIND

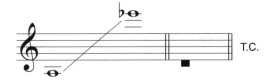

ALTO CLARINET in F (BASSETT-HORN)
Fr. Cor de Basset;
It. Corno di Bassetto;
Ger. Bassetthorn

T.C.

A BASS CLARINET
Fr. Clarinette Basse en La;
It. Clarone in La;
Ger. Bassklarinette in A

T.C.

E♭ ALTO CLARINET
Fr. Clarinette Alto en Mi♭;
It. Clarinetto Alto in Mi♭;
Ger. Altklarinette in Es

T.C.

E♭ CONTRA BASS CLARINET
Fr. Clarinette Contrabasse en Mi♭;
It. Clarino Contrabasso in Mi♭;
Ger. Kontrabassklarinette in Es

T.C.

B♭ BASS CLARINET
Fr. Clarinette Basse en Si♭;
It. Clarone in Si♭;
Ger. Bassklarinette in B

T.C.

B♭ CONTRA BASS CLARINET
Fr. Clarinette Contrabasse en Si♭;
It. Clarino Contrabasso in Si♭;
Ger. Kontrabassklarinette in B

T.C.

SAXOPHONES

E♭ SOPRANINO SAXOPHONE
It. Sassophone Sopranino in Mi♭;

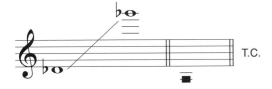

T.C.

C SOPRANO SAXOPHONE
Fr. Saxophone Dessus en Ut;
It. Sassophone Soprano in Do;
Ger. Sopran Saxophon in C

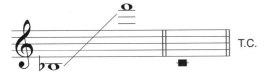

T.C.

B♭ SOPRANO SAXOPHONE
Fr. Saxophone Dessus en Si♭;
It. Sassophone Soprano in Si♭;
Ger. Sopran Saxophon in B

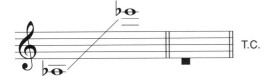

T.C.

E♭ ALTO SAXOPHONE
Fr. Saxophone Haut-Contre en Mi♭;
It. Sassophone Alto in Mi♭;
Ger. Alt Saxophon in Es

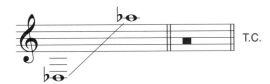

T.C.

C MELODY SAXOPHONE
Fr. Saxophone Melodie en Ut;
It. Sassophone Melodie in Do;
Ger. Saxophon Melodia in C

T.C.

B♭ TENOR SAXOPHONE
Fr. Saxophone Tenor en Si♭;
It. Sassophone Tenore in Si♭;
Ger. Tenor Saxophon in B

T.C.

E♭ BARITONE SAXOPHONE
Fr. Saxophone Bariton en Mi♭;
It. Sassophone Baritono in Mi♭;
Ger. Bariton Saxophon in Es

T.C.

B♭ BASS SAXOPHONE
Fr. Saxophone Basse en Si♭;
It. Sassophone Basso in Si♭;
Ger. Bass Saxophon in B

T.C.

HORNS

FRENCH HORN in B♭
Fr. Cor-a-pistons en Si♭;
It. Corno Ventile in Si♭;
Ger. Ventilhorn in B

T.C.
& B.C.

FRENCH HORN in E♭
Fr. Cor-a-pistons en Mi♭;
It. Corno Ventile in Mi♭;
Ger. Ventilhorn in Es

T.C.
& B.C.

FRENCH HORN in F
Fr. Cor-a-pistons en Fa;
It. Corno Ventile in Fa;
Ger. Ventilhorn in F

T.C.
& B.C.

DOUBLE HORN (in B♭ & F)

T.C.
& B.C.

MELLOPHONE in E♭ (E♭ Alto, *Coiled*)
(Concert Horn)

T.C.

COR de CHASSE in E♭ (Natural Horn)

T.C.
& B.C.

(Also, in D)

TRUMPETS

Bb PICCOLO TRUMPET
Fr. Petite Trompette en Si♭;
It. Ottavino Tromba in Si♭;
Ger. Kleine Trompete in B

Bb TRUMPET
Fr. Trompette en Si♭;
It. Tromba in Si♭;
Ger. Trompete in B

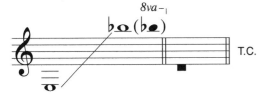

Eb TRUMPET *(Soprano or Piccolo)*
Fr. Trompette en Mi♭;
It. Tromba in Mi♭;
Ger. Trompete in Es

D TRUMPET
Fr. Trompette en Re;
It. Tromba in Re;
Ger. Trompete in D

C TRUMPET
Fr. Trompette en Ut;
It. Tromba in Do;
Ger. Trompete in C

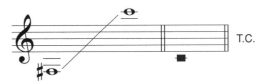

G TRUMPET
Fr. Trompette en Sol;
It. Tromba in Sol;
Ger. Trompete in G

F TRUMPET *(Soprano)*
Fr. Trompette en Fa;
It. Tromba in Fa;
Ger. Trompete in F

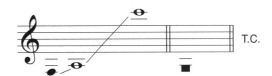

F TRUMPET *(Alto)*
Fr. Trompette en Fa;
It. Tromba in Fa;
Ger. Trompete in F

SLIDE TRUMPET

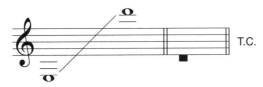

14

A TRUMPET
Fr. Trompette en La;
It. Tromba in La;
Ger. Trompete in A

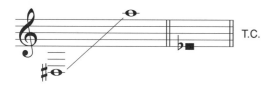

T.C.

D BACH TRUMPET (No valves)

T.C.

BASS TRUMPET *in C*
Fr. Trompette Basse en Ut;
It. Tromba Bassa in Do;
Ger. Basstrompete in C

T.C.
or B.C.

C BACH TRUMPET (No valves)

T.C.

BASS TRUMPET in B♭
Fr. Trompette Basse en Si♭;
It. Tromba Bassa in Si♭;
Ger. Trompete in B

T.C.
or B.C.

COACH HORN (in B♭)

T.C.

HERALD TRUMPET (in B♭)
(Commonly known as Aida Trumpet)

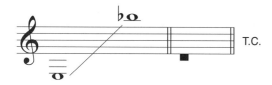

T.C.

POSTHORN (in A)

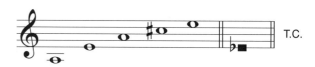

T.C.

15

CORNETS - FLUGELHORNS

Eb PICCOLO CORNET

Fr. Petite Cornet en Mib;
It. Ottavino Cornetto or Cornetta in Mib;
Ger. Kleines Cornett in Es

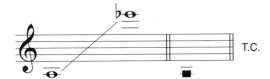

ALTO HORN in Eb (Alto Cornet)
(Eb Alto, *Bell Front or Bell Up*)
Fr. Bugle Alto en Mib;
It. Flicorno Alto in Mib;
Ger. Althorn or Altkornett in Es

Bb CORNET
Fr. Cornet en Sib;
It. Cornetto or Cornetta in Sib;
Ger. Cornett in B

Eb SOPRANO FLUGELHORN
Fr. Bugle Dessus en Mib;
It. Flicorno Soprano in Mib;
Ger. Sopran Flügelhorn in Es

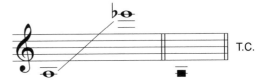

A CORNET
Fr. Cornet en La;
It. Cornetto or Cornetta in La;
Ger. Cornett in A

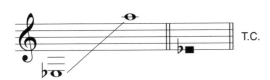

Bb FLUGELHORN
Fr. Bugle en Sib;
It. Flicorno in Sib;
Ger. Flügelhorn in B

ALTO HORN in F (Alto Cornet)
Fr. Bugle Alto en Fa;
It. Flicorno Alto in Fa;
Ger. Althorn or Altkornett in F

Eb ALTO FLUGELHORN
Fr. Bugle Haut-Contre (Bugle Alto) en Mib;
It. Flicorno Alto in Mib;
Ger. Alt Flügelhorn in Es

BUGLES

B♭ BUGLE
Fr. Bugle en Si♭;
It. Tromba in Si♭;
Ger. Bügelhorn in B

T.C.

KEYED BUGLE in C

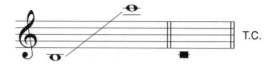

T.C.

G BUGLE
Fr. Bugle en Sol;
It. Tromba in Sol;
Ger. Bügelhorn in G

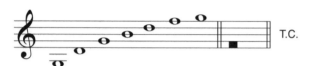

T.C.

KEYED BUGLE in B♭

T.C.

BUGLE in G (Slide *(crook)* to F)
Military Regulation

T.C.

KEYED BUGLE in A

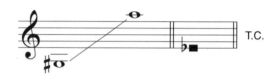

T.C.

SOPRANO PISTON BUGLE in G to D (Rotary Valve to F♯)

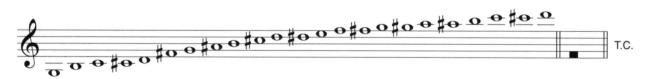

T.C.

SOPRANO PISTON BUGLE in G to D (Rotary Valve to F)

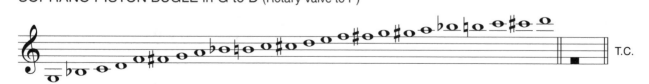

T.C.

SAXHORNS

Invented by Adolphe Sax in 1843 by the application of the
valve-mechanism to Keyed-Bugles and Ophicleides.

E♭ SOPRANINO SAXHORN
Fr. Petite Saxhorn, Petite Bugle á Pistons en Mi♭;
Ger. Piccolo in Es
*(E♭ Piccolo Cornet, pg. 15)

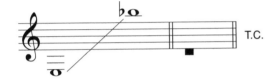

B♭ TENOR SAXHORN
Fr. Baryton en Si♭;
Ger. Tenorhorn in B, Bassflügelhorn
*(Baritone in B♭, Tenor Horn, pg. 19)

B♭ SOPRANO SAXHORN
Fr. Contralto Saxhorn en Si♭;
Ger. Flügelhorn in B
*(B♭ Cornet, pg. 15)

B♭ BASS SAXHORN
Fr. Tuba Basse en Si♭;
Ger. Euphonium, Baryton, Tenorbass in B
*(Euphonium, pg. 19)

E♭ ALTO SAXHORN
Ger. Althorn in Es
*(Alto Horn, Alto Cornet, pg. 15)

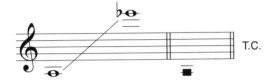

E♭ BASS SAXHORN
Fr. Bombardon en Mi♭;
*(E♭ Military Tuba, pg. 19)

B♭ CONTRA BASS SAXHORN
Fr. Bombardon en Si♭;
Ger. Kontrabasstuba in B
*(BB♭ Military Tuba, pg. 19)

*This denotes the contemporary counterpart.

TROMBONES

SOPRANO TROMBONE in B♭
(Slide Trumpet)

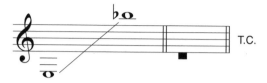

T.C.

BASS TROMBONE in F
Fr. Trombone Basse en Fa;
It. Trombone Basso in Fa;
Ger. Bassposaune in F

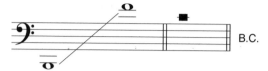

B.C.

ALTO TROMBONE in E♭
Fr. Trombone Haute-Contre en Mi♭;
It. Trombone Alto in Mi♭;
Ger. Altposaune in Es

A.C.
B.C.
& T.C.

BASS TROMBONE in E♭
Fr. Trombone Basse en Mi♭;
It. Trombone Basso in Mi♭;
Ger. Bassposaune in Es

B.C.

TENOR TROMBONE in B♭
Fr. Trombone Tenor;
It. Trombone Tenore;
Ger. Tenorposaune

B.C.
&
Ten.C.

CONTRA BASS TROMBONE in B♭
Fr. Trombone Contrebasse;
It. Trombone Contrabasso;
Ger. Kontrabass Posaune

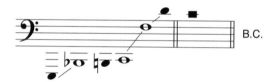

B.C.

BASS TROMBONE in B♭
Fr. Trombone Basso en Si♭;
It. Trombone Basso in Si♭;
Ger. Bassposaune in B

B.C.
&
Ten.C.

CONTRA BASS TROMBONE in F

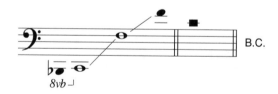

B.C.

BASS TROMBONE in G
Fr. Trombone Basso en Sol;
It. Trombone Basso in Sol;
Ger. Bassposaune in G

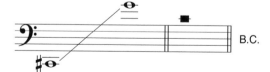

B.C.

VALVE TROMBONE in B♭ (3 valves)
Fr. Trombone a Pistons;
It. Trombone Ventile;
Ger. Ventilposaune

B.C.
& Ten.C.

VALVE TROMBONE in B♭
(7 cylinder)

B.C.
&
Ten.C.

TUBAS

BARITONE (in B♭) (3 valves)
Fr. Bugle Ténor en Si♭, Barytone en Si♭,
It. Flicorno Tenore in Si♭;
Ger. Tenorhorn in B

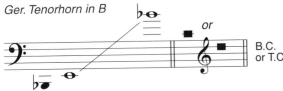

B.C.
or T.C.

ORCHESTRA TUBA (in F)

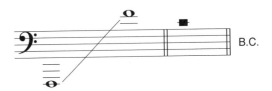

B.C.

EUPHONIUM (in B♭) (4 valves)
Fr. Basse a Pistons,
It. Eufonio;
Ger. Baryton

B.C.
or T.C.

E♭ MILITARY TUBA
(Helicon, Sousaphone)

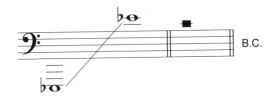

B.C.

FRENCH PETITE TUBA in C
Fr. Petite Tuba en ut

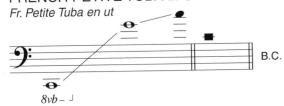

B.C.

BB♭ & CC MILITARY TUBA
(Helicon, Sousaphone)

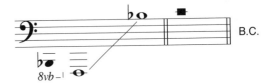

B.C.

TENOR TUBA (in B♭)

B.C.

CONTRA BASS TUBA
Ger. Kontrabasstuba

B.C.

This is the four-valve Tuba that was introduced by Wagner to complete the group of so-called "Wagner Tubas" which was comprised of two high and two low *Modified Horns* and one true Tuba.

TUBEN
(Wagner Tubas)

TENOR TUBEN in B♭

T.C.
or B.C.

BASS TUBEN in F

T.C.
or B.C.

Modified Horns

HARMONICAS

Note: These instruments represent the basic group of professional Harmonicas. They are not to be confused with the numerous instruments manufactured in various sizes and keys (chromatic and non-chromatic), usually for amateur or specialized use.

HARMONICA (Standard Chromatic)

HARMONICA (4 Octave Chromatic "64")

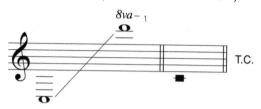

CHORD HARMONICA (Maj., Min., Dom. 7th, Aug. and Dim. Chords)

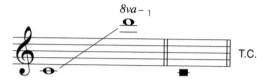

BASS HARMONICA (Standard)
(Due to limited technical facility, rapid chromatic changes should be avoided.)

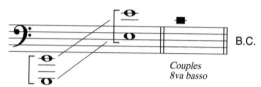

OCARINAS

RECORDERS

Note: Chromatic intervals are not easily played.

SOPRANINO RECORDER (in F)
Fr. Flûte à Bec Sopranino en Fa;
It. Flauto Dolce, Sopranino in Fa;
Ger. Sopranino-Blockflöte in F

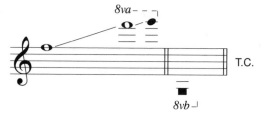

TENOR RECORDER
Fr. Flûte à Bec Ténor;
It. Flauto Dolce, Tenore;
Ger. Tenorblockflöte

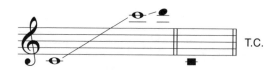

SOPRANO RECORDER (Descant)
Fr. Flûte à Bec Dessus;
It. Flauto Dolce, Soprano;
Ger. Sopranblockflöte

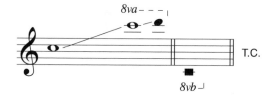

BASS RECORDER (in F)
Fr. Flûte à Bec Basse en Fa;
It. Flauto Dolce, Basso in Fa;
Ger. Bassblockflöte in F

ALTO RECORDER (in F) (Treble)
Fr. Flûte à Bec Haute-Contre en Fa;
It. Flauto Dolce, Alto in Fa;
Ger. Altblockflöte in F

GREAT BASS RECORDER (in C)
Fr. Flûte à Bec en Ut;
It. Flauto Dolce, Basso in Ut;
Ger. Gross-bassblockflöte in C

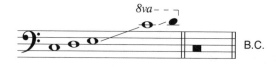

PERCUSSION

ALMGLOCKEN, TUNED (Alpine/Swiss Cowbells)

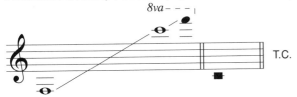

T.C.

ALUPHONE

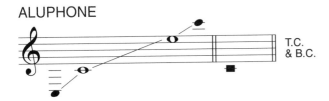

T.C. & B.C.

ANGKLUNG (Metal) *(Sounds in 2 octaves)*

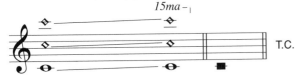

T.C.

ANGKLUNG (Bamboo) *(Sounds in 1 or possibly 2 octaves)*

T.C. & B.C.

ANVILS *(Chromatic)*

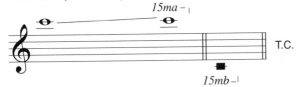

T.C.

BELL PLATES

T.C. & B.C.

BELL LYRA *(Upright Band Glock)*

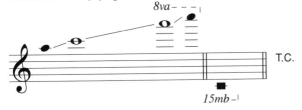

T.C.

BELLS, ORCHESTRA, PARSIFAL
Fr. Carillon or Jeu de Timbre;
It. Campanetta;
Ger. Glockenspiel

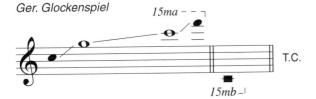

T.C.

BOO BAMS

T.C. & B.C.

BOOMWHACKERS

T.C. & B.C.

BULB HORNS *(Chromatic)*

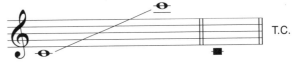

T.C.

CHIMES (TUBULAR BELLS)
Fr. Cloches;
It. Campane or Campanelle;
Ger. Glocken

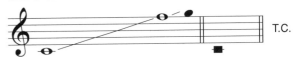

T.C.

CHIMES (TUBULAR BELLS), BASS

B.C.

CIMBALOM

T.C. & B.C.

COWBELLS *(Chromatic)*

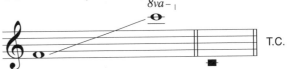

T.C.

CROTALES (Tuned Cymbals)

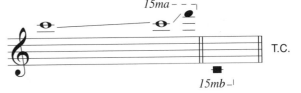

T.C.

DESK BELLS *(Chromatic)*

T.C.

DOWEL-A-PHONE (Rosewood Dowels)

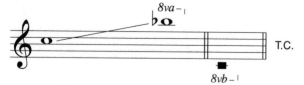

T.C.

FLAPAMBA

T.C.
& B.C.

GLOCKENSPIEL (Orch. Bells)
Fr. Carillon or Jeu de Timbre;
It. Campanetta;
Ger. Glockenspiel

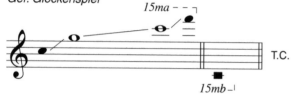

T.C.

GONGS, TUNED

T.C.
& B.C.

HANDBELLS *(Chromatic)*

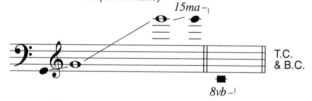

T.C.
& B.C.

JAPANESE TEMPLE BELLS (Rin Bowls)

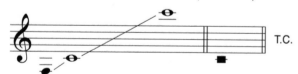

T.C.

LOG DRUMS *(Chromatic)*

B.C.

MARIMBA

T.C.
& B.C.

MARIMBA, BASS
Fr. Marimba Basse;
It. Marimba Basso;
Ger. Bassmarimba

B.C.

MARIMBA, Buzz (Zapotecano)

T.C.
& B.C.

MARIMBA, GLASS

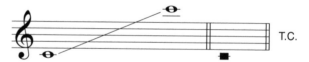

T.C.

MBIRA, ARRAY

T.C.
& B.C.

MBIRA, KALIMBA *(Chromatic)*

T.C.

MBIRA: KALIMBA (17 Note Treble) *This instrument has fixed playable notes. It is also known as a "Thumb Piano".*

T.C.

MBIRA: KALIMBA (15 Note Alto)

T.C.

MARIMBA, OCTARIMBA *(Sounds in octaves)*

T.C. & B.C.

MARIMBA, STEEL

8va

T.C.

MARIMBA, STONE

T.C. & B.C.

ROTO TOMS

T.C. & B.C.

RUB RODS (Round)

8va

T.C.

8vb

RUB RODS (Square)

8va

T.C.

8vb

SATELLITE DRUMS

T.C.

SLEIGH BELLS *(Chromatic)*

T.C.

SONG BELLS

8va

T.C.

STEEL DRUMS, TENOR (Lead Pan, Soprano Pan)

8va - - -

T.C.

STEEL DRUMS (Double Seconds)

T.C.

STEEL DRUMS (Cello Pans)

B.C.

STEEL DRUMS (Bass Pans)

B.C.

TEMPLE BLOCKS, TUNED

T.C.

TIMPANI (Kettle Drum)
Fr. Timbales;
It. Timpani;
Ger. Pauken

*20"

B.C.

*23"

B.C.

24"

B.C.

25"

B.C.

*26"

B.C.

*The Standard Set in the U.S.A. is 20", 23", 26", 29", 32".

continued

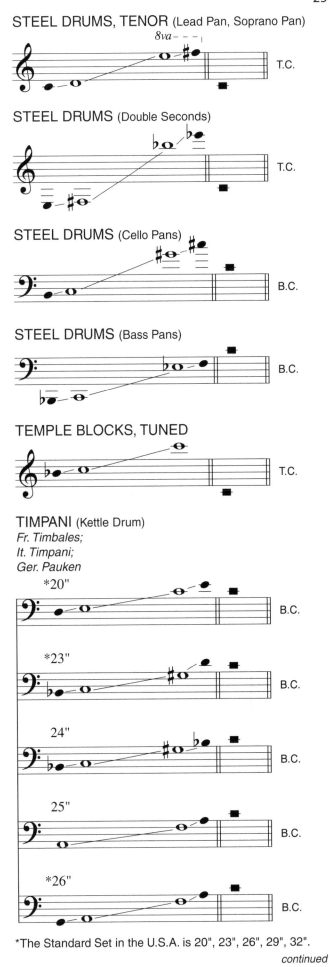

27"

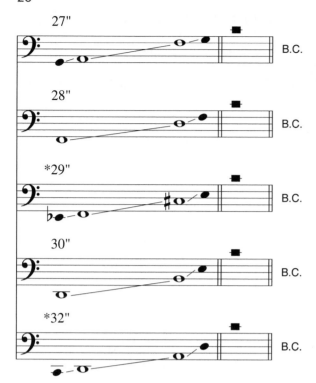

B.C.

28"

B.C.

*29"

B.C.

30"

B.C.

*32"

B.C.

*The Standard Set in the U.S.A. is 20", 23", 26", 29", 32".

TOY PIANO

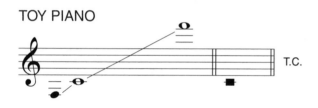

T.C.

TUBAPHONE

8va –

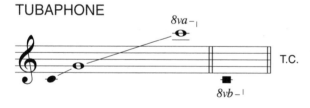

T.C.

8vb –

TUBAPHONE (Brass Tube Gamelon)

8va –

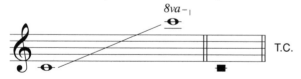

T.C.

TUBAPHONE (Galvanized Pipe Gamelon)

8va –

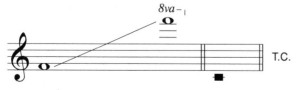

T.C.

TUBAPHONE, TUBE BELLS, VISCOUNT BELLS

8va –

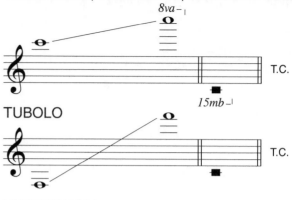

T.C.

15mb –

TUBOLO

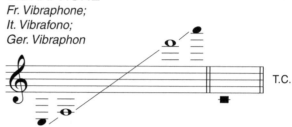

T.C.

VIBRAPHONE

Fr. Vibraphone;
It. Vibrafono;
Ger. Vibraphon

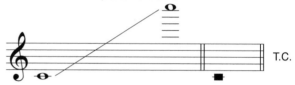

T.C.

VIBRAPHONE, SOPRANO

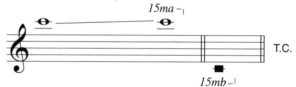

T.C.

WOOD BLOCKS, PICCOLO

15ma –

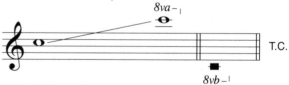

T.C.

15mb –

WOOD BLOCKS, TUNED

8va –

T.C.

8vb –

XYLOPHONE

Fr. Xylophon or Claquebols;
It. Xilofono;
Ger. Xylophon, Strohfiedel or Holzharmonika

15ma –

T.C.

8vb –

XYLORIMBA

15ma –

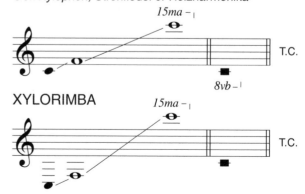

T.C.

Percussion Instruments courtesy of Dan Savell
Los Angeles Percussion Rentals

KEYBOARD INSTRUMENTS

ACCORDION-Standard
(Chord Buttons - Maj. - Min. - Dom. 7th - Dim.)
Fr. Accordeon;
It. Accordeon;
Ger. Accordeon, Akkordion or Ziehharmonika

ACCORDION-Free Bass System
(No Chord Buttons)

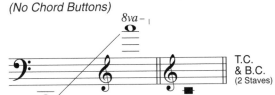

MUSETTE ACCORDION
Fr. Musette Accordeon;
It. Musette Accordeon;
Ger. Musette Accordeon

BASS ACCORDION
Fr. Accordeon Basse;
It. Accordeon Basso;
Ger. Bass Accordeon

CELESTA

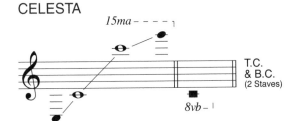

CLAVINET, Hohner D6

CONCERTINA

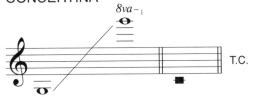

KEYBOARD GLOCKENSPIEL

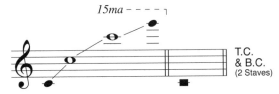

NOVACHORD

PIANO
Fr. Piano, Pianoforte;
It. Piano, Pianoforte;
Ger. Klavier, Pianoforte

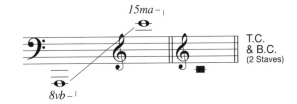

ELECTRIC PIANO

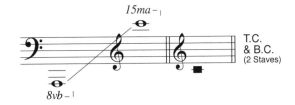

HARPSICHORD (Bach Model, double keyboard)
Fr. Clavecin;
It. Arpicordo, Clavicembalo;
Ger. Kielflügel

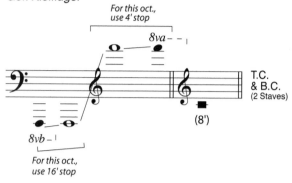

The 16', 8' and 4' stops can be used individually, simultaneously, or coupled in any combination.

SMALL HARPSICHORD (single keyboard)
Fr. Petite Clavecin;
It. Ottavino Arpicordo, Ottavino Clavicembalo;
Ger. Kleiner Kielflügel

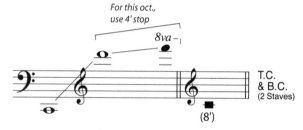

The keyboard (8') and 4' stops can be coupled or used individually.

CLAVICHORD
Fr. Clavicorde;
It. Clavicordo;
Ger. Klavichord, Klavier

CALLIOPE

(This instrument is not manufactured to particular specifications.)

CLAVIETTA

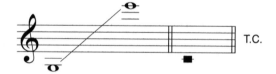

This instrument has a mouthpiece and piano-type keyboard.

ELECTRIC HARPSICHORD (BALDWIN)

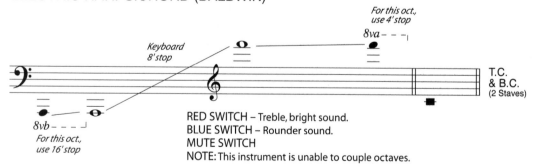

RED SWITCH – Treble, bright sound.
BLUE SWITCH – Rounder sound.
MUTE SWITCH
NOTE: This instrument is unable to couple octaves.

VIBRACHORD® & HARP CELESTA (Maas-Rowe)

The tone selector of the Vibrachord® varies the tone coloring in the amplifier to give a variety of effects. The Harp Celesta, which has no tone selector, has a straight Vibraharp tone.

SOLOVOX

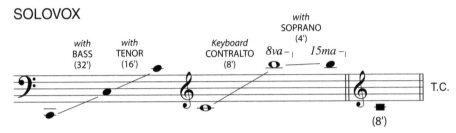

The Bass (32'), Tenor (16'), Contralto (8') and Soprano (4') controls can be used individually, simultaneously, or coupled in any combination.

ORGANS

Note: The following Organ range notations represent the *written ranges only*. The possible sounding ranges are obtained by using the available stops of the particular instrument.

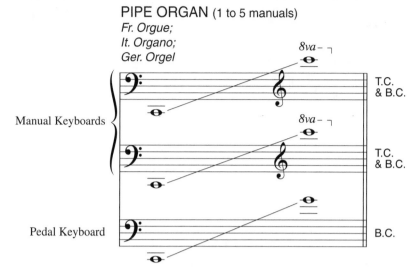

PIPE ORGAN (1 to 5 manuals)
Fr. Orgue;
It. Organo;
Ger. Orgel

Manual Keyboards

Pedal Keyboard

NAMES OF THE MANUAL KEYBOARDS

The Manual Keyboards are arranged on the instrument in numerical order, with the 1st Manual being closest to the performer.

2 Manual	FRENCH	ITALIAN	GERMAN
Ist man. Great	I Grand orgue	I Principale	I Hauptwerk
2nd man. Swell	II Positit au récit	II Organo di coro	II Brustwerk
			Positiv or Schwellwerk,
			or:
			I Positiv
			II Hauptwerk

3 Manual			
Ist man. Choir (Ch.)	I Grand orgue	I Organa di coro	I Hauptwerk
2nd man. Great (Gt.)	II Positif	II Principale	II Positiv
3rd man. Swell (Sw.)	III Récit	III Organo d'espressione	III Schwellwerk;
	or:		*or:*
	I Positif		I Rückpositiv
	II Grand orgue		II Hauptwerk
	III Récit		III Brustwerk;
			or:
			I Brustwerk
			II Hauptwerk
			III Oberpositiv

4 Manual			
Ist man. Choir	I Grand orgue	I Organa di coro	I Brustwerk
2nd man. Great	II Positif	II Principale	II Hauptwerk
3rd man. Swell	III Récit	III Organo d'espressione	III Positiv
4th man. Solo	IV Solo	IV Organo d'assolo	IV Schwellwerk;
	or:		*or:*
	I Ruckpositif		I Rückpositiv
	II Grand orgue		II Hauptwerk
	III Positif		III Oberwerk
	IV Récit		IV Brustwerk;
			or:
			I Hauptwerk
			II Positiv
			III Schwellwerk
			IV Solowerk

5 Manual			
Ist man. Choir	I Grand choeur	I Principale	I Hauptwerk
2nd man. Great	II Grand orgue	II Organa di coro	II Brustwerk
3rd man. Swell	III Bombarde	III Organo d'espressione	III Schwellwerk
4th man. Solo	IV Positif	IV Organo d'assolo	IV Solowerk
5th man. Echo	V Récit	V Organo d'eco	V Echowerk

(NOTE: The manual arrangement of the 5-manual organ varies in different countries and schools.)

WRITTEN ORGAN REGISTRATIONS

In writing for the organ, due to the extreme differences in individual instruments, registration beyond the general classes of stops *(shown in italics, pgs. 32 and 33),* dynamic levels, and pitches other than 8' on the manuals, or 16' on the pedals, is usually not desirable.

A register (stop) is a series of organ pipes, from the largest to the smallest, homogeneous in timbre and intensity, each pipe corresponding to a key on the manual. A drawstop or stop-key on the console brings the series into play.

The relative pitch of registers is expressed in terms of feet. The pitch of the eight foot (8') register is that of the piano. The fundamental pitch of the manual-keyboards is 8'; that of the pedal-keyboard is 16'.

A unison stop produces the normal note of the key played, e.g. 32', 16', 8', 4', 2', 1'.

A *mutation stop* is a register which does not produce the normal note of the key played, but a natural harmonic of that note, used for creating or modifying timbre.

The *mixture ranks* are the combinations of upper harmonics, varying in number according to the number of ranks used. The number is usually indicated on the stop. Because of the almost inaudible high pitch of the harmonics of the upper notes, manufacturers must make special modifications after a certain point on the keyboard. These modifications are known as 'breaks' or 'returns', and are made at the discretion of the individual manufacturer.

CHART OF UNISON AND MUTATION STOPS

STOP in feet	Pitch in relation to the note played	HARMONIC SERIES					
		32'	16'	8'	4'	2'	1'
32'	two octavos lower	1st					
16'	one octave lower	2nd	1st				
10 2/3'	a perfect fourth lower	3rd					
8'	normal pitch of note played	4th	2nd	1st			
*6 2/5'	a major third higher	5th					
5 1/3'	a perfect fifth higher	6th	3rd				
*4 4/7'	a harmonic seventh higher	7th					
4'	one octave higher	8th	4th	2nd	1st		
*3 1/5'	one octave and a third higher		5th				
2 2/3'	one octave and a fifth higher		6th	3rd			
*2 2/7'	one octave and a harmonic seventh higher		7th				
2'	two octaves higher		8th	4th	2nd	1st	
1 3/5'	two octaves and a third higher			5th			
1 1/3'	two octaves and a fifth higher			6th	3rd		
*1 1/7'	two octaves and a harmonic seventh higher			7th			
1'	three octaves higher			8th	4th	2nd	1st

*Rare

The tremolo or tremulant causes a pulsation in the wind supply to the pipes associated with a specific manual-keyboard, thus producing a vibrato effect. Separate tremolos are provided for each manual-keyboard.

The manual-keyboards can be coupled together or to the pedal-keyboard. These are known as *manual* and *pedal couplers.* They may be at 8' (unison), 4' (octave), or 16' (sub-octave) pitches on the manuals, and 8' and 4' pitches on the pedals.

The Swell-Pedal activates a shutter on the pipe enclosure, creating a controlled crescendo or diminuendo. There may be separate Swell-Pedals for each manual-keyboard.

The Register Crescendo Pedal gradually brings into play all of the registers, from the softest to the full power of the instrument, overriding the drawstop or stop key controls. The Sforzando Reversible thumb or toe piston instantly brings into play the full power of the instrument, overriding the drawstop or stop key controls, and remaining effective until pushed a second time.

STOPS IN COMMON USE
MANUAL STOPS

Foundation Stops (French: *Fonds*) include Principals (Diapasons), Flutes and String stops of unison pitches, all of which are voiced toward the Principal timbre, the characteristic sound of the concert pipe organ which resembles somewhat the orchestral unison of French Horn *mf*, Trombone in cup mute *mf*, Bassoon *p*, and Bass Flute *f*, all sounding middle C.

Principal (Open Diapason) (French: *Montre, Prestant*; German: *Prinzipal*; Italian: *Principale*) *mf-f* 16', 8', 4'; Quint *mf-f* 5-1/3'; Octave *mf-f* 4'; Twelfth *mp-f* 2:2/3'; Fifteenth or Super-Octave *mp-f* 2'; Sifflet or Siffote *mf* 1'; Dulciana or Dolce *pp-mp* 16', 8', 4', 2-2/3', 2'.

Mixture (French: *Mixture, Fourniture, Plein Jeu, Cornet*; German: *Mixtur, Scharf, Kornett, Zimbel*; Italian: *Ripieno*) *mf-ff* 2 to 7 ranks (usually expressed in Roman numerals), usually 3 to 4 ranks and of Principal timbre. The above stops are used in combination to build the Principal or Diapason Chorus, the basic organ sound.

Chorus Reeds (French: *Anches*): Trumpet *f-ff* 16', 8', 4'; Trompette *f-ff* 16', 8', 4'; Tromba or Trombone or Bombarde or Ophicleide *ff* 16', 8', 4'; Tuba *ff-fff* 16', 8', 4'; Clarion *mf-fff* 4'; Oboe or Hautboy (non imitative) *mp-f* 8', 4'. As their names indicate, these stops have a muffled to brilliant brassy timbre with extremely rapid incisive attack.

Chorus reeds plus Mixtures are used to build the Reed of secondary Chorus on large concert (and church) organs.

Open Flutes (French: *Flute*; German: *Flöte*; Italian: *Flauto*): Flute *p-f* 16', 8', 4', 2', 1'; Flauto Mirabilis *f-ff* 8'; Concert Flute *mf-f* 8'; Melodia *mp-mf* 8'; Hohlflöte *mp-f* 8'; Waldflote *mp-mf* 8', 4'; Blockflöte *mp-f* 4', 2'; Flute Harmonique *mf-f* 8', 4'; Harmonic Piccolo *mf-f* 2'; Piccolo or Flautino *mp-f* 2'; Spitzflöte (has a horn-like edge to timbre) *mp-mp* 8', 4'. These stops have a round, open tone somewhat like the orchestral Flute or Recorder.

Stopped Flutes (Stopped Diapasons) (French: *Bourdon*; German: *Gedeckt*): Stopped Flute *p-f* 16', 8', 4', 2'; Chimney Flute (French: *Flute a Cheminee*; German: *Rohrflöte, Rohrgedeckt*) *mp-mf* 16', 8', 4', 2'. These stops have hollow flute tone similar to the Ocarina, Panpipes, Slide Whistle, or Cuckoo Call.

Quintadenas or *Quintatens* *mp-f* 16', 8', 4', 2' are a unique organ timbre composed of stopped pipes overblown so as to sound their twelfths as loud as the fundamentals. The nearest orchestral equivalent would be the E♭ Clarinet in its lowest register, played as softly as possible.

Strings (French: *Gambe, Viole*; German: *Geigen*): *pp-f* 16', 8', .4'; Salicional *mp-mf* 16', 8', 4'; Salicet *mp-mf* 4'; Viola da Gamba or Gamba *mp-mf* 8'; Cello or Violone *mf-f* 16', 8'; Viola *mp-mf* 8', 4'; Violina *mp-mf* 4', 2'; Muted Viol or Muted String *pp-p* 8', 4'; Aeoline (the softest stop on any organ) *ppp* 8'. These stops have a bright to extremely keen and thin tone similar to orchestral strings and are slow to respond in attack.

Gemshorn *p-f* 8', 4' and *Erzähler* *mp-mf* 8', 4'. These stops have a hybrid flute-string timbre, and are usually quite prompt in speech.

Celestes: stops tuned slightly sharp or flat so as to produce a wavering or beating ensemble or vibrato effect when combined with a unison stop. They may occur in any of the quieter voices, most commonly as a String or Viol Celeste (French: *Voix Celeste*) 8'; Dulciana Celeste or Unda Maris 8', 4'; Flute, Celeste 8'; Gemshorn Celeste 8'; Kleiner Erzähler 8'; Cello Celeste 8'. Muted Strings 8', 4'.

Mutations: usually of Flute timbre: Gross Nasard *mf-f* 5-1/3'; Gross Tierce *mp-f* 3-1/5'; Nasard *mp-f* 2-2/3'; Tierce *p-mf* 1-3/5'; Larigot *p-f* 1-1/3'. These stops are combined with unison stops to add tone color for solo registrations.

continued

Solo Reeds: Clarinet *mp–f* 16', 8'; Krummhom or Cromorne *mp–f* 8'; Cor Anglais *mf* 8';Vox Humana *pp–mp* 8'; Oboe (imitative) *mp–mf* 8'; French Horn *mf–f* 8'. These stops are more or less imitative, with the possible exception of the Vox Humana, a stop always used with tremulant, which was intended to evoke the effect of a choir humming nasally.

Percussions: Chimes (tubular bells) (8') range: 2 octaves G3–G5; Harp (8' or 4') or Celesta (4') or Celesta Sub (8') range: 4 octaves C3-C7, metal bars with resonators. These stops are quite similar to the Tubular Chimes and Celesta of the orchestra.

PEDAL STOPS

The pedal stops are similar in quality to manual stops of the same names.

Principal (Open Diapason) *mf–ff* 32', 16', 8', 4'; Choral Bass *f–fff* 4'; Octave *mf–ff* 8'; Quint *mf–ff* 10-2/3', 5-1/3'; Dulciana *pp–mp* 16', 8'.

Mixtures: 2 to 5 ranks of Principal timbre.

The above stops are used in combination to build the principal Pedal Chorus.

Chorus Reeds: Bombarde *ff–fff* 32', 16', 8', 4'; Trombone *f–ff* 16', 8'; Tromba *f–ff* 8'; Clarion *f–fff* 4'; Bassoon or Fagott *mp–f* 16', 8'.

Open Flutes: Grossflöte or Flute *mf–ff* 8', 4'.

Stopped Flutes: Bourdon *mp–ff* 32', 16', 8', 4'; Gedeckt *pp–mf* 16', 8'.

Quintadenas or *Quintatens:* *mp–f* 32', 16', 8'.

Strings: Violone or Violoncello *mp–f* 32', 16', 8'; Salicional *mp–mf* 16'.

Celestes, Mutations, Solo Reeds and Percussions are usually playable on the pedal keyboard only by coupling from the manual divisions.

THEATER PIPE ORGAN

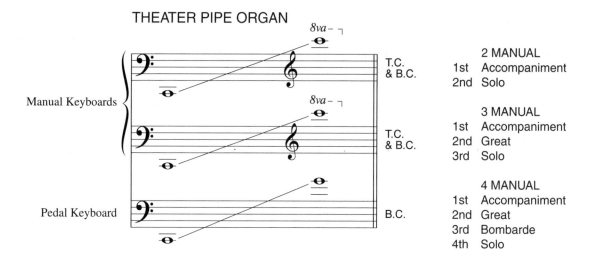

Manual Keyboards

Pedal Keyboard

T.C. & B.C.

T.C. & B.C.

B.C.

2 MANUAL
1st Accompaniment
2nd Solo

3 MANUAL
1st Accompaniment
2nd Great
3rd Solo

4 MANUAL
1st Accompaniment
2nd Great
3rd Bombarde
4th Solo

THEATER PIPE ORGAN

The written and sounding ranges of the Theater Pipe Organ are essentially the same as the Concert Pipe Organ. The essential difference is that a relatively small number of sets or ranks of pipes (registers) are employed, and usually, each is available at a great variety of pitches on all keyboards. These registers are voiced to extreme differences in timbre, and the mutations are derived from the Tibia Clausa (a very heavy stopped flute), and from the Concert Flute (a plain open flute of wood and of moderate intensity).

On the Theater Pipe Organ, the *tremolo* or *vibrato* is most extreme in its action. Separate vibratos are usually provided for the Tibia Clausa, the Vox Humana, the Main or Foundation registers, and the Solo registers. Each register is associated with either the Main or the Solo expression chambers (more in some large instruments); they do not have a 'home' keyboard at the console.

Couplers are held to a minimum, since most registers are already independently available at a great variety of pitches on all keyboards.

Cb.	REGISTERS Name	TIMBRE	PITCHES
S	Tibia Clausa	Stopped Flute ff	16', 8', 5-1/3', 4', 2-2/3', 2'
M	Diaphonic Diapason	Principal ff	16', 8', 4', Pedal (32')
S	Horn Diapason	Principal mf	16', 8', 4'
M	Concert Flute	Open Flute mf	16', 8', 4', 2-2/3', 2', 1-3/5'
S	Solo String	String f	16', 8', 4'
S	Solo String Celeste	String f (♮)	16', 8', 4'
M	Salicional or Viole d'Orchestre	String mf	16', 8', 4', 2'
M	Voix Celeste or Viole Celeste	String mf (♮)	8', 4'
M	Dulciana	Principal p	8', 4'
S	English Horn (Posthorn)	Chorus Reed ff	16', 8'
M	Tuba	Chorus Reed ff	16', 8', 4'
S	Trumpet	Chorus Reed f	16', 8', 4'
S	Saxophone	Solo Reed mf	16', 8'
S	Oboe Horn	Solo Reed mf	8', 4'
M	Clarinet	Solo Reed mf	16', 8'
S	Orchestral Oboe	Solo Reed mf	8'
S	Kinura	Solo Reed mf	8'
M	Vox Humana	Solo Reed p	16', 8', 4'

Cb. = Chamber
M = Main (Left)
S = Solo (Right)

continued

There are many tuned and non-tuned percussion registers that are composed of the actual orchestral instruments, fitted with electro-pneumatic actions. Those usually encountered are:

CHRYSOGLOTT (4') G3-G7, essentially a Celesta.
HARP (4') C5-C7, a single-stroke Marimba.
MARIMBA (4') C3-C7, reiterating action.
XYLOPHONE (2') C4-C7, reiterating action.
GLOCKENSPIEL (2') G5-C8, single-stroke Orchestra Bells.
ORCHESTRA BELLS (2') G5-C8, reiterating action.
CHIMES (8') G3-G5.
PIANO, with Mandolin Effect, (16', 8', 4'), standard compass.
TUNED SLEIGH BELLS (8') C4-C6, reiterating action.
BASS DRUM, (on Pedal).
KETTLE DRUM, (Bass Drum with continuous roll), (on Pedal).
CRASH CYMBAL, (on Pedal).
CYMBAL, (on Pedal).
SNARE DRUM, (Accomp.).
TOM-TOM, (Accomp.).
TAMBOURINE, (Accomp.).
CASTANETS, (Accomp.)
TRIANGLE, (Great).
WOOD BLOCK, (Accomp.).
SAND BLOCK, (Accomp.).

On some instruments, a large group of sound effects is present, such as: *Auto Horn, Locomotive Whistle, Steamboat Whistle, Siren, Fire Gong, Door Bell, Thunder, Surf, Bird Whistle, Horse's Hoofs, Gong, Grand Crash* or *Crockery Smash, Wind,* etc. These are usually controlled by thumb or toe buttons, independent of the keyboards.

The Swell-Pedals have a much more extreme effect on the volume of the Theater Pipe Organ than on the concert (church) instrument. Two Swell-Pedals are usually provided, one each for the Solo (S) and Main (M) chambers.

A Register Crescendo Pedal, which is usually supplied, brings on all the registers from soft to loud, in sequence, overriding the stop key register controls.

Thumb pistons are provided under each manual keyboard for the rapid changing of registrations for that keyboard. Toe pistons are provided for changing pedal registrations.

ELECTRIC ORGANS
(other than Hammond Organs)

These instruments have various controls, similar to those found on the Pipe Organ.

Due to the numerous models manufactured to different specifications, the following represents only the '2 manual instruments' that may be most available.

CHURCH & CONCERT MODELS

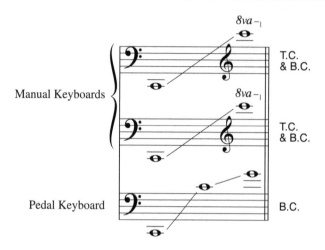

SPINET MODELS

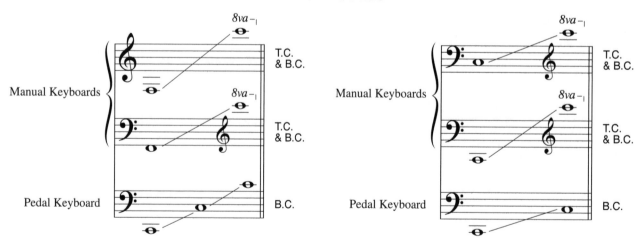

HAMMOND ORGANS

The unique feature of the Hammond Organs is the harmonic drawbar. This device replaces the use of "stops", such as, "diapason", "flute", "strings", etc., and furnishes the fundamentals and harmonics from which these effects and numerous others can be created.

Each harmonic is available in eight stages of intensity (volume), the eight numbers being marked on the drawbars. These numbers are used to indicate the preferred tone qualities so that they can be exactly duplicated when desired.

There are nine drawbars in each group that control the upper and lower manuals of the Console Models. The Spinet Models M-100 and L-100 series have the complete group of nine drawbars that control the upper manual. However, the M-100 series has eight drawbars for the lower manual, and the L-100 series has only seven.

In addition to the manual drawbars, the Console Models have two pedal drawbars. The left drawbar controls the low, deep quality (16 ft. pitch) and the right drawbar adds brightness of tone one octave higher (8 ft. pitch). The Spinet Models have only one pedal drawbar which controls an already combined pedal tone.

The following illustration shows the drawbars in relationship to Pipe Organ terminology.

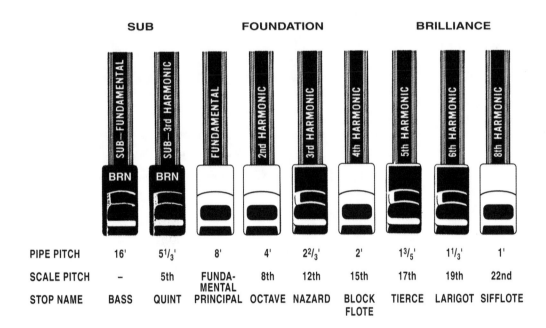

	SUB		FOUNDATION				BRILLIANCE		
	SUB—FUNDAMENTAL (BRN)	SUB—3rd HARMONIC (BRN)	FUNDAMENTAL	2nd HARMONIC	3rd HARMONIC	4th HARMONIC	5th HARMONIC	6th HARMONIC	8th HARMONIC
PIPE PITCH	16'	$5\frac{1}{3}$'	8'	4'	$2\frac{2}{3}$'	2'	$1\frac{3}{5}$'	$1\frac{1}{3}$'	1'
SCALE PITCH	–	5th	FUNDA-MENTAL	8th	12th	15th	17th	19th	22nd
STOP NAME	BASS	QUINT	PRINCIPAL	OCTAVE	NAZARD	BLOCK FLOTE	TIERCE	LARIGOT	SIFFLOTE

By permission of The Hammond Organ Company

THE COLORS OF THE DRAWBARS

The significance of the colors of the black, white and brown drawbars on the Hammond Organ, is shown in the following illustrations.

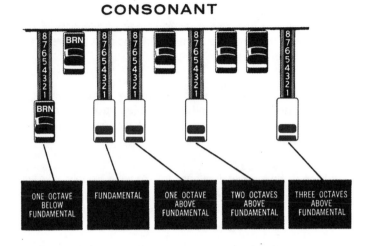

WHITE DRAWBARS

The first white drawbar for each manual represents the fundamental tone. All the other white drawbars are octave intervals or harmonics of the fundamental tone. The tonal brilliance is greatly increased by adding white drawbars but the harmonics added are always in 'consonance'.

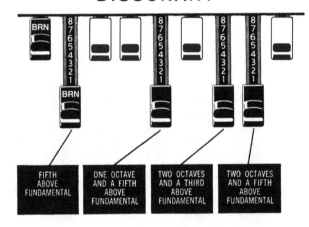

BLACK DRAWBARS

The black drawbars represent the dissonant (discordant) harmonics which are also necessary in building rich tone colors. In general, the black drawbars should not be emphasized too strongly above the white drawbars. If a black drawbar is to be emphasized, it is a good rule to use adjacent white drawbars to strengths within two steps of the black drawbar.

By permission of The Hammond Organ Company

BROWN DRAWBARS

In addition to the white and black drawbars, there are two brown drawbars. *(These do not exist in the group controlling the lower manual of the Spinet Models.)* These two drawbars produce "sub-octave" effects. The first brown drawbar is the sub-octave of the fundamental and the second brown drawbar is the sub-octave of the third harmonic. These are used to add depth and richness to many combinations. They also increase the range of the keyboard by one octave, since a solo registration for "8 foot", or normal pitch, can be set up using the first brown drawbar as the fundamental, and played one octave higher.

continued

HAMMOND CONSOLE MODELS
(Concert Model, Home Model,
C-3 Model & A-100 Series)

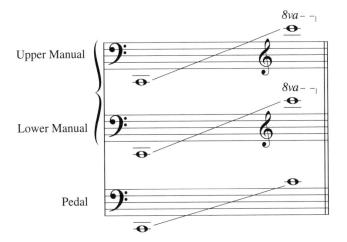

HAMMOND SPINET MODELS
(Models M-100 & , L-100 Series)

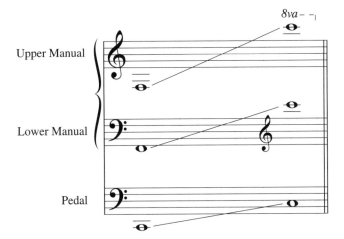

HAMMOND CONSOLE MODELS   HARMONIC DRAWBARS

UPPER MANUAL   **LOWER MANUAL**

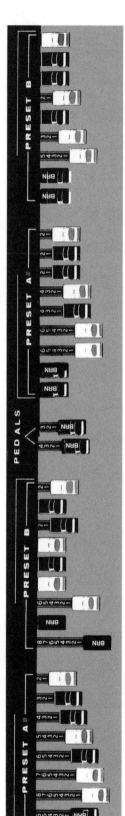

By permission of The Hammond Organ Company

In the above illustration you will notice that there are two groups of harmonic drawbars (instead of one) for each manual. The purpose is to allow prepared combinations to be ready and waiting for use. With two groups of drawbars for each manual, it becomes necessary to have control keys (known as *pre-set keys*) to select the group wanted.

There are twelve black and white (reversed keyboard color) pre-set keys ranging from C through B. These keys are located to the left of each manual keyboard. The first on each manual is a cancel key. The next nine keys, C# through A, are preset to the tones most often used by organists. The last two keys on each manual, A# and B (sometimes called "adjust" keys) are actually on-and-off switches to control the tones created and set up on the four groups of drawbars.

The white keys are the solo, and single-tone qualities, the black ones are the ensemble qualities. The softer tones are at the left, gradually growing louder to the right. They are always used one at a time; and *cannot be used in combination.* Pressing one key releases all other keys.

THE CONTROL TABLETS

THE VOLUME AND VIBRATO CONTROLS

There are three control tablets – VOLUME *normal-soft,* VIBRATO SWELL *off-on,* VIBRATO GREAT *off-on,* and a

six-position switch controlling the degrees of VIBRATO (*V-1, V-2, V-3*) and VIBRATO CHORUS (*C-1, C-2, C-3*).

The VIBRATO SWELL tablet turns the VIBRATO or VIBRATO CHORUS on or off on the "swell" or upper manual. The VIBRATO GREAT does the same on the "great" or lower manual.

PERCUSSION

There are four control tablets – PERCUSSION *on-off,* PERCUSSION VOLUME *soft-normal,* PERCUSSION DECAY *fast-slow,* and PERCUSSION HARMONIC SELECTOR *second-third.*

The position of the HARMONIC SELECTOR tablet determines the pitch at which the percussion tone sounds. When set at *SECOND,* the pitch is up one octave with respect to the Fundamental Drawbar; when set at *THIRD,* the pitch is up an octave and a fifth.

THE SOLO PEDAL UNIT

Exclusive to the Concert Model (RT-3) of the Hammond Organ. This unit augments the 16 ft. and 8 ft. pedal drawbar tones at all pitches; 32 ft., 16 ft., 8ft., 4 ft., 2 ft., and 1 ft. A knob controls the volume.

Example of indication for settings of *Pre-Set Keys; Drawbars; Percussion and Vibrato* tablets.

UPPER MANUAL: Ⓑ 80 0800 000   **PEDAL 54, PERCUSSION:** ON, NORMAL, SLOW, SECOND, Vibrato V-3.
LOWER MANUAL: A♮ 00 4434 113

continued

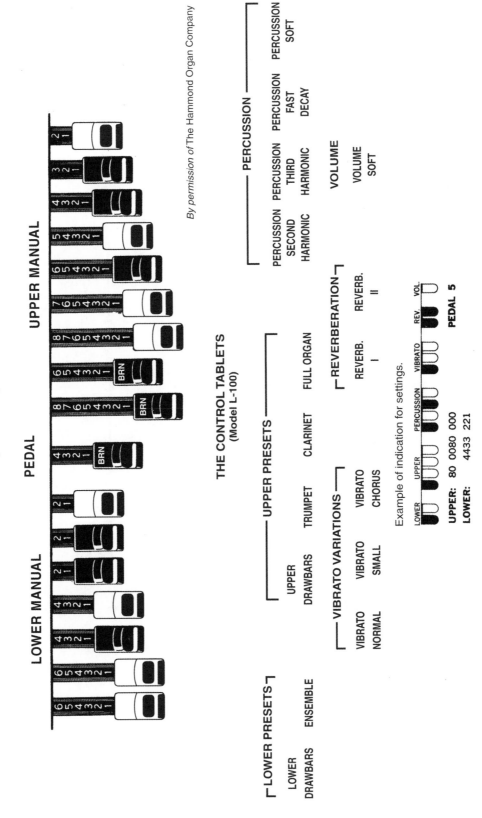

HARMONIC DRAWBARS
(Model L-100)

UPPER MANUAL

PEDAL

LOWER MANUAL

By permission of The Hammond Organ Company

THE CONTROL TABLETS
(Model L-100)

LOWER PRESETS

LOWER DRAWBARS — ENSEMBLE

UPPER PRESETS

UPPER DRAWBARS — TRUMPET — CLARINET — FULL ORGAN

VIBRATO VARIATIONS

VIBRATO NORMAL — VIBRATO SMALL — VIBRATO CHORUS

PERCUSSION

PERCUSSION SECOND HARMONIC — PERCUSSION THIRD HARMONIC — PERCUSSION FAST DECAY — PERCUSSION SOFT

VOLUME

VOLUME SOFT

REVERBERATION

REVERB. I — REVERB. II

Example of indication for settings.

LOWER   UPPER   PERCUSSION   VIBRATO   REV.   VOL.

PEDAL 5

UPPER: 80 0080 000
LOWER: 4433 221

continued

HAMMOND SPINET ORGANS

HARMONIC DRAWBARS
(Model M-100)

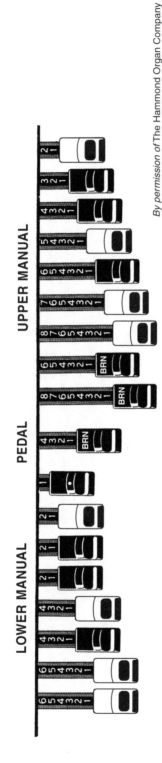

LOWER MANUAL   PEDAL   UPPER MANUAL

By permission of The Hammond Organ Company

Note: The eighth drawbar for the lower manual (black with white dot) combines two additional upper harmonics to add richness and brilliance to certain tones.

THE CONTROL TABLETS
(Model M-100)

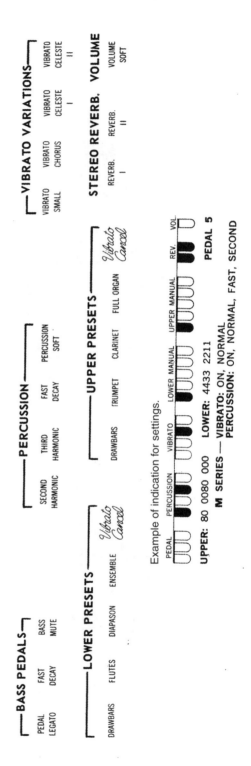

BASS PEDALS
PEDAL LEGATO | FAST DECAY | BASS MUTE

LOWER PRESETS
DRAWBARS | FLUTES | DIAPASON | ENSEMBLE | *Vibrato Cancel*

PERCUSSION
SECOND HARMONIC | THIRD HARMONIC | FAST DECAY | PERCUSSION SOFT

UPPER PRESETS
DRAWBARS | TRUMPET | CLARINET | FULL ORGAN | *Vibrato Cancel*

VIBRATO VARIATIONS
VIBRATO SMALL | VIBRATO CHORUS | VIBRATO CELESTE I | VIBRATO CELESTE II

STEREO REVERB.
REVERB. I | REVERB. II

VOLUME
VOLUME SOFT

Example of indication for settings.

PEDAL | PERCUSSION | VIBRATO | LOWER MANUAL | UPPER MANUAL | REV | VOL | PEDAL 5

UPPER: 80 0080 000   LOWER: 4433 2211

M SERIES — VIBRATO: ON, NORMAL
PERCUSSION: ON, NORMAL, FAST, SECOND

HAMMOND ORGAN PRE-SET CHART

UPPER MANUAL

PRE SET KEYS	DRAWBAR SETTING	TONE QUALITY	LOUDNESS VALUE
C		Cancel	
C♯	00 5320 000	Stopped Flute	*pp*
D	00 4432 000	Dulciana	*ppp*
D♯	00 8740 000	French Horn	*mf*
E	00 4544 222	Salicional	*pp*
F	00 5403 000	Flutes 8' & 4'	*p*
F♯	00 4675 300	Oboe Horn	*mf*
G	00 5644 320	Swell Diapason	*mf*
G♯	00 6876 540	Trumpet	*f*
A	32 7645 222	Full Swell	*ff*
A♯	Adjust harmonic drawbars in 1st Group, Upper Manual		
B	Adjust harmonic drawbars in 2nd Group, Upper Manual		

LOWER MANUAL

PRE SET KEYS	DRAWBAR SETTING	TONE QUALITY	LOUDNESS VALUE
C		Cancel	
C♯	00 4545 440	Cello	*mp*
D	00 4423 220	Flute & String	*mp*
D♯	00 7373 430	Clarinet	*mf*
E	00 4544 220	Diapason, Gamba and Flute	*mf*
F	00 6644 322	Great, no reeds	*f*
F♯	00 5642 200	Open Diapason	*f*
G	00 6845 433	Full Great	*ff*
G♯	00 8030 000	Tibia Clausa	*f*
A	42 7866 244	Full Great with 16'	*fff*
A♯	Adjust harmonic drawbars in 1st Group, Lower Manual		
B	Adjust harmonic drawbars in 2nd Group, Lower Manual		

SOME DISTINCTIVE DRAWBAR REGISTRATIONS
(for all Hammond Organs)

Tibia 16'................... 72 0020 000	Tibia 8' 00 8240 000	Flute 4'..................... 00 0803 030
Bourdon 16'............ 54 3100 000	Concert Flute 8' 00 6421 000	Piccolo 4' 00 0600 000
Diapason 16' 64 3322 000	Diapason 8'.............. 00 5642 110	Octave 4' 00 0545 321
Solo Strings 16' 25 4421 000	Solo Strings 8' 00 2366 542	Solo Strings 4' 00 0436 555
Contra Viol 16' 24 3210 000	Viol d'Orchestre 8' ... 00 2444 322	Viol 4'...................... 00 0344 232
Contra Celeste 16'... 23 4321 000	Viole Celeste 8'........ 00 2323 211	Octave Celeste 4' ... 00 0324 220
Vox Humana 16' 14 3110 000	Vox Humana 8' 00 3400 332	Vox Humana 4' 00 0433 042
Oboe Horn 16' 47 5430 000	Oboe Horn 8' 00 4763 000	Oboe Horn 4'.......... 00 0606 310
Saxophone 16' 27 3210 000	Saxophone 8'........... 00 2478 500	Clarion 4' 00 0515 230
Clarinet 16' 35 2000 000	Clarinet 8' 00 8382 700	Tibia 2'..................... 00 0006 001
English Horn 16'...... 25 3442 100	English Horn 8' 00 3577 540	Piccolo 2' 00 0005 111
Ophicleide 16'.......... 47 7600 000	Tuba 8' 00 5680 400	Twelfth 00 0060 020

FLUTE TONES

FLUTE TONES
00 6200 000

LIGHT CONCERT FLUTE
00 3700 000

SEVERAL FLUTES TOGETHER
00 7605 004

REED TONES

TYPICAL REED EFFECT
OBOE 00 4632 100

TRUMPET-TYPE TONE
00 6876 540

VOICE-LIKE EFFECT
00 1200 432

CLARINET TONE
00 7272 420

CHORUS REED EFFECT
with sub-octave
76 7777 765

FOUNDATION (Diapason) TONES

PHONON TYPE DIAPASON
00 5521 000

DIAPASON CHORUS
54 5444 222

FULL ORGAN EFFECT
54 7878 766

THEATRE ORGAN EFFECT
57 8766 553 full vibrato

XYLOPHONE TONE
00 0800 080 no vibrato

STRING TONES

VIOLIN TONE
00 4345 554 full vibrato

A STRING SECTION
12 3333 444 string chorus effect

HARMONIUM

Written range

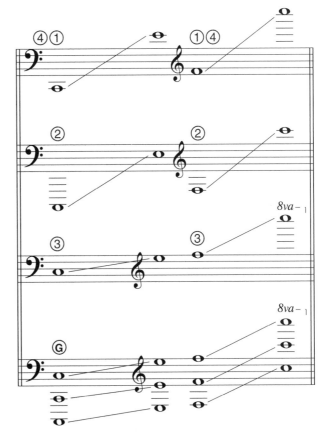

Note:
The ① of the left hand is for the accompaniment.
The ① of the right hand is adapted for light and
smooth passages.

① ④ = 8'
② = 16'
③ = 4'

REGISTERS OF THE LEFT HAND

⓪	⑤	④	③	②	①
Forte de Basses	Violoncelle	Basson	Clairon	Bourdon	Cor Anglais

MIDDLE REGISTERS

EM	G	E
Piano de Basses	Gradn Jeu	Expression

REGISTERS OF THE RIGHT HAND

①	②	③	④	⑤	⓪
Flute	Klarinette	Fifre	Hautbois	Musette	Forte des Dessus

CARILLONS

Carillon music is usually written on two staves, treble and bass clefs. When the range of the instrument starts from middle C, both staves are notated in treble clef.

(Cast Bells)

A Carillon is a set of fixed, cast bells, referred to as *carillonic bells,* that are usually activated by a keyboard mechanism. Since there is no set number of cast bells in each Carillon, a standard range cannot be shown. The playing range can vary from one octave, diataonic, to four octaves, chromatic, and the performer can control the impact of each strike.

Due to the lack of standardization, it is necessary to check each instrument's sounding range to determine the key in which the instrument is tuned. The pitch of the Carillon is determined by the largest (lowest sounding) bell, which is usually called C on the keyboard.

Although harmony can be played on most Carillons, some English carillonic bells are cast for the sole purpose of being played individually or as units used in change-ringing and the playing of peals. These bells, sometimes known as *English Pealing Bells,* are not suitable for playing harmony because of the dissonance of their partial series.

The partial series, sounding from the strike tone of a particular cast bell, may vary according to individual opinion. However, its basic characteristic is to sound the minor third partial. It should also be noted that the basic difference between the partial series of a bell-tone and that of the natural harmonic series is that the partials of the bell-tone sound *below* as well as *above* the fundamental.

The following shows the partial series (generally accepted) for the harmony-playing English, Flemish, French, German and American Carillons:

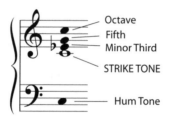

ELECTRONIC CARILLONS

This instrument is an electronic unit with a tone source derived from 25 or more small, solid, metal rods that are arranged in chromatic sequence. It can be operated by a piano-type keyboard or an automatic playing device.

It should be noted that the resultant tone of an Electronic Carillon differs from that of a cast bell Carillon. This is explained by the fact that the physical structure of the metal rod makes it impossible to have an identical series of partials to those of the cast bell. Therefore, a tuning process is used, and the tuning processes of the partials vary according to the invention of the individual manufacturer.

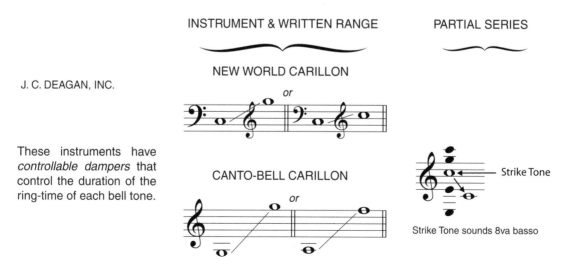

continued

MAAS-ROWE CARILLONS

This instrument has an automatic key selector that connects proper major and minor bells to the lower keyboard. This permits playing from one keyboard. On the 122 and 100 bell models, a one-octave pedal clavier is added for playing the deepest-toned bells.

UPPER *(Maj.)* **KEYBOARD**
(Notation: ◁)

LOWER *(Min.)* **KEYBOARD**
(Standard Notation)

SYMPHONIC CARILLON®

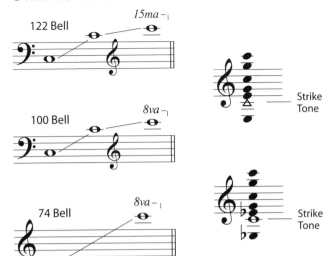

Due to the subtone (below pitch harmonic), a Carillon tone impresses the ear as sounding one octave lower than played.

STROMBERG-CARLSON COMPANY

The MECHLIN CARILLON has a direct, piano-type action keyboard to create a playing technique similar to that used with a cast bell carillon.

MECHLIN CARILLON

LOUVAIN CARILLON

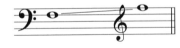

TELEMATICS INC.

This instrument produces the traditional grandeur of the Flemish bells and, at the flick of a switch, the lighter, crisper English bells. A dual keyboard system allows the player to simulate the playing of cast bells. The lower manual hits with the normal intensity of strike and the upper manual has a softer strike.

FLEMISH MASTER CARILLON

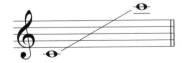

ELECTRO-ACOUSTICAL CARILLONS

SCHULMERICH CARILLONS, INC.

All Schulmerich carillons use precision-tuned, miniature bell-tone generators, struck by metal hammers, as their tone sources. This action duplicates that of a metal clapper striking a cast bronze bell.

The Carillon Americana® Bells are played from a 2 manual organ type console with full pedal clavier built to AGO standards. The 305 Bell instrument is comprised of the following sets of chromatically tuned bells:

- 61 Flemish Bells
- 61 Harp Bells
- 61 Celesta Bells
- 61 Quadra Bells
- 61 Minor Tierce Bells

The Arlington® Carillon has individual expression pedal controls for tenor and treble bells which provide a wide dynamic range for solo and accompaniment.

The Coronation® Carillon has a patented Decadence Control which provides the diminishment of tone without a throttling effect of dampers.

CARILLON AMERICANA®
Bells Instrument

ARLINGTON® CARILLONS
(Flemish Type)

Multi-toned AMERICANA®
Bells Instrument

These instruments may consist of 2, 3, 4, or 5 octaves of Flemish tuned "Arlington" carillon bells, Harp bells and/or Celesta bells, making it available in 50 to 183 bell ranges. Each set of bells may be manually played from its own respective keyboard,- or in combinations from two or more keyboards.

CORONATION® CARILLON
(English Type)

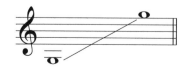

Strike Tone
plus Prime

STRING INSTRUMENTS

BAGLAMA (Greece)

T.C.

BAGLAMA (Turkey) *Duzeni Tuning*

T.C.

BAJO QUINTO (Mexico)

B.C.

BAJO SEXTO (Mexico)

B.C.

BALALAIKAS

BALALAIKA, PRIMA (Russia)

T.C.

BALALAIKA, ALTO (Russia)

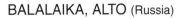

T.C.

BALALAIKA, SECUNDA (Russia)

T.C.

BALALAIKA, BASS (Greece)

B.C.

BALALAIKA, CONTRA BASS (Greece)

B.C.

50

BANDOLA ANDINA COLUMBIANA (Columbia)

BANDOLA GUYANESE (Venezuela)

BANDOLA LLANERA (Venezuela)

BANDOLA ORIENTAL (Venezuela)

BANDOLIM (Brazil)

BANDOLIN (Ecuador)

BANDURRIA (Philippines)

BANDURRIA (Spain)

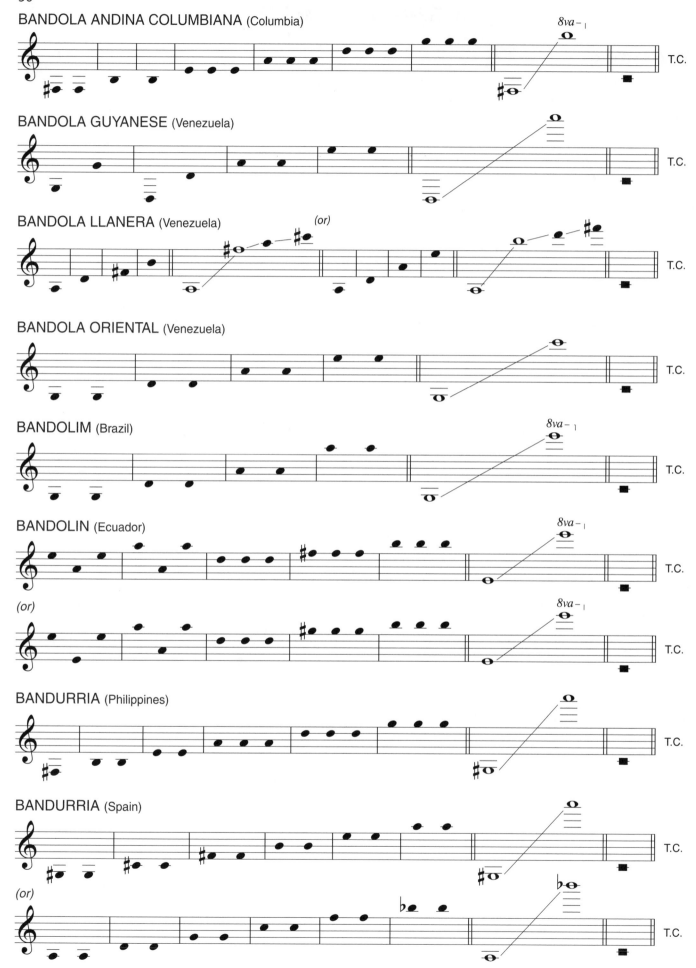

BANJOS

TENOR, 4 String, Traditional Jazz, 17 & 19 Frets

T.C.

12 String, 22 Frets

T.C.

COUNTRY, JAZZ, ROCK, 6 String, 22 Frets

T.C.

PLECTRUM, 4 String, 22 Frets

T.C.

PARLOR, BLUEGRASS, 5 String, 22 Frets, Open String Tuning

T.C.

LONG NECK, 5 String, Pop, Folk, 25 Frets

T.C.

Courtesy of Deering Banjo Company

52

BASS, 4 & 5 STRING *(Double Bass)*
Fr. Contre Basse;
It. Contrabasso;
Ger. Kontrabass

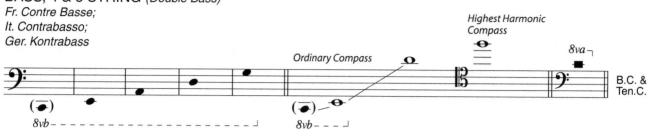

Ordinary Compass
Highest Harmonic Compass
8va
B.C. & Ten.C.
8vb
8vb

BIWA, CHIKUZEN, 4 STRING (Japan)

B.C.

BIWA, CHIKUZEN, 5 STRING (Japan)

B.C.

BIWA, NISHIKI, 4 STRING (Japan)

(or)

B.C.

BIWA, SATSUMA, 4 STRING (Japan)

B.C.

(or)

B.C.

BORDONUA, 6 STRING (Puerto Rico)

B.C.

BORDONUA, 10 STRING (Puerto Rico)

T.C. & B.C.

BOUZOUKIS

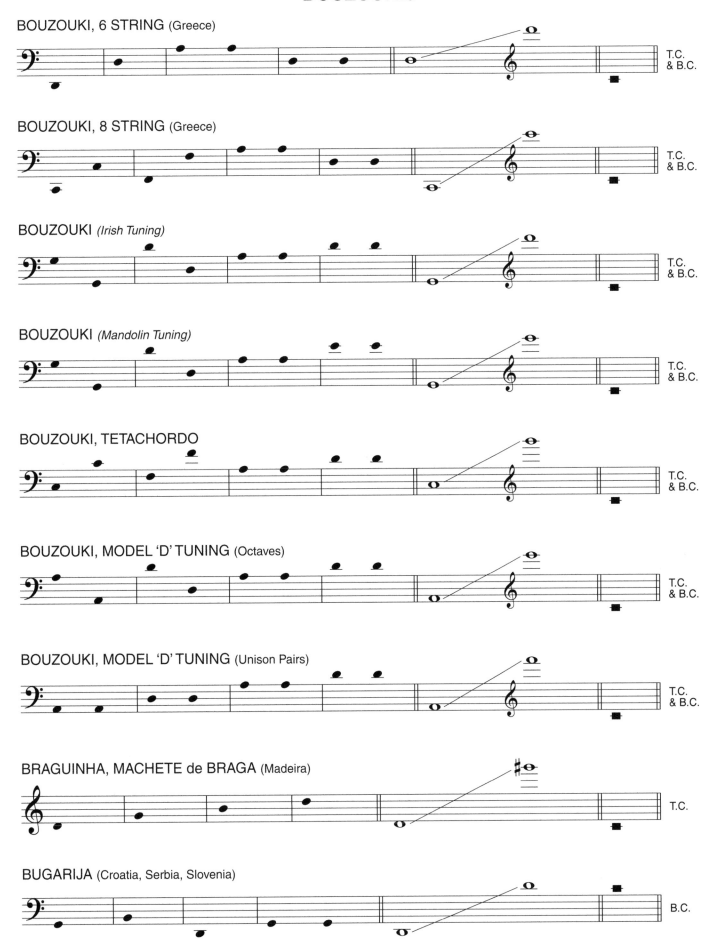

54

CAK (Indonesia)

CAVAQUINHO (Portugal, Brazil)

CELLO
Fr. Violoncelle;
It. Violoncello;
Ger. Violoncello

CETERA (Corsica, France)

CHARANGO, C6 TUNING (Bolivia, Peru)

CHARANGON, F6 TUNING (Andes, Peru)

CHILLADOR (South America)

CHITARRA BATTENTE (Southern Italy)

CHONGURI, FRETTED or FRETLESS (Georgia)

(or)

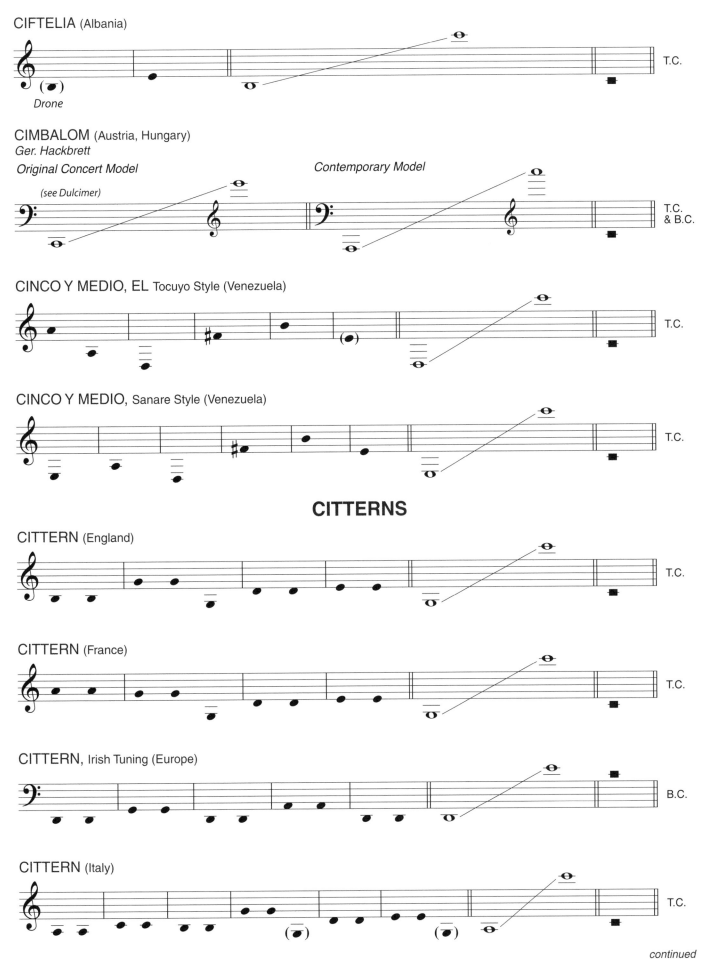

CIFTELIA (Albania)

Drone

CIMBALOM (Austria, Hungary)
Ger. Hackbrett
Original Concert Model
Contemporary Model
(see Dulcimer)

CINCO Y MEDIO, EL Tocuyo Style (Venezuela)

CINCO Y MEDIO, Sanare Style (Venezuela)

CITTERNS

CITTERN (England)

CITTERN (France)

CITTERN, Irish Tuning (Europe)

CITTERN (Italy)

continued

CITTERN, Mandolin Low C Tuning (Europe)

B.C.

CITTERN, Modal D Tuning (Europe)

B.C.

CROWTH (Wales) *A Bowed Instrument*

T.C.

CUATRO, CUBANO (Cuba)

B.C.

CUATRO (Puerto Rico)

T.C.

CUATRO (Venezuela)

T.C.

CUK (Indonesia)

T.C.

57

CUMBUS, "STANDARD" FRETLESS (Turkey)

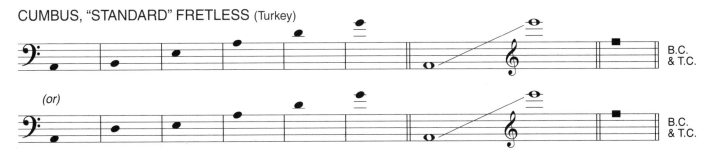

B.C.
& T.C.

(or)

B.C.
& T.C.

There are several types of Cumbus. Each of which (except the "Standard") sort of mimics another type of instrument such as the Mandolin, Ukulele, Tanbur, Saz, Guitar, etc., by using the tuning of that instrument.

CUMBUS, FRETTED (Turkey)

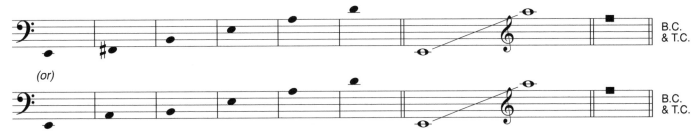

B.C.
& T.C.

(or)

B.C.
& T.C.

DOMRAS (Russia)
(Note: A 4th string is sometimes added, tuned a 4th lower than the lowest string.)

PICCOLO DOMRA

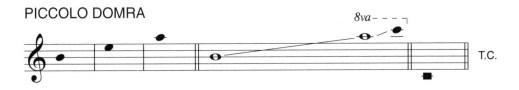

T.C.

PRIMA DOMRA

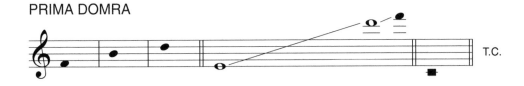

T.C.

ALTO DOMRA

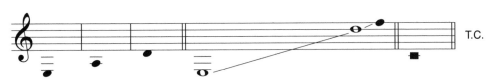

T.C.

TENOR DOMRA

T.C.
& B.C.

BARITONE DOMRA

B.C.

BASS DOMRA

B.C.

CONTRA BASS DOMRA

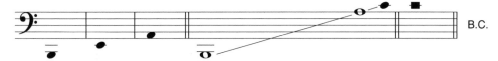

B.C.

DULCIMER, APPALACHIAN

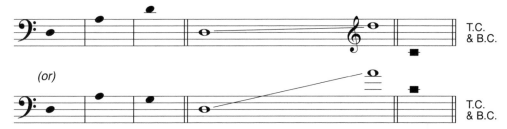

T.C.
& B.C.

(or)

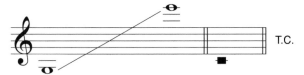

T.C.
& B.C.

DULCIMER, HAMMERED
Model 13/12
The treble bridge contains 13 courses, with position markings for the D4, G4, C5, and F5 keys.
The bass bridge contains 12 courses, with position markings for the G3, C4, F4, and B♭4 keys.

T.C.

Model 16/15
Model 16/15 has an extended range with an added treble bridge marking for the A3 key
and the extended bass bridge marking of the D3 key.

T.C.
or B.C.

Model 19/18
Model 19/18 (the largest model) has an extended range with an added treble bridge
marking for the E3 key and the extended bass bridge marking of the A2 key.

T.C.
or B.C.

These instruments feature movable bridges that enable the top two courses of each bridge to be sharped
(converting to chromatic) by sliding the bridge segments toward the center of the instruments.

By permission of June Apple Dulcimers, Accokeek, MD. USA

HAMMERED DULCIMER TUNING CHART

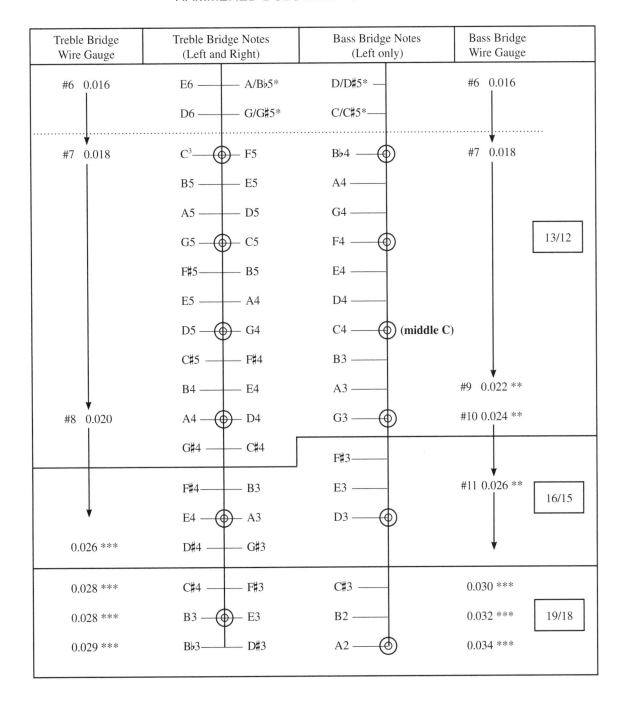

Treble Bridge Wire Gauge	Treble Bridge Notes (Left and Right)		Bass Bridge Notes (Left only)	Bass Bridge Wire Gauge
#6 0.016	E6	A/B♭5*	D/D♯5*	#6 0.016
	D6	G/G♯5*	C/C♯5*	
#7 0.018	C³	F5	B♭4	#7 0.018
	B5	E5	A4	
	A5	D5	G4	
	G5	C5	F4	13/12
	F♯5	B5	E4	
	E5	A4	D4	
	D5	G4	C4 (middle C)	
	C♯5	F♯4	B3	
	B4	E4	A3	#9 0.022 **
#8 0.020	A4	D4	G3	#10 0.024 **
	G♯4	C♯4	F♯3	
	F♯4	B3	E3	#11 0.026 ** 16/15
	E4	A3	D3	
0.026 ***	D♯4	G♯3		
0.028 ***	C♯4	F♯3	C♯3	0.030 ***
0.028 ***	B3	E3	B2	0.032 *** 19/18
0.029 ***	B♭3	D♯3	A2	0.034 ***

* The notes indicated by "*" at the top of both bridges are capable of being sharped 1/2 step via moveable bridge segments. Both notes are shown, separated by a "/".

**Brass wire   ***Wound wire   ⊙ Bridge markings

By permission of June Apple Dulcimers, Accokeek, MD, USA

PIANO DULCIMER - Model PD40

T.C.
& B.C.

This model has three bridges arranged in the piano dulcimer format. Fully chromatic for its 3 1/2 octave range, with bridge cap markers that mimic the pattern of white and black notes on the piano.

TUNING & STRINGING DIAGRAM

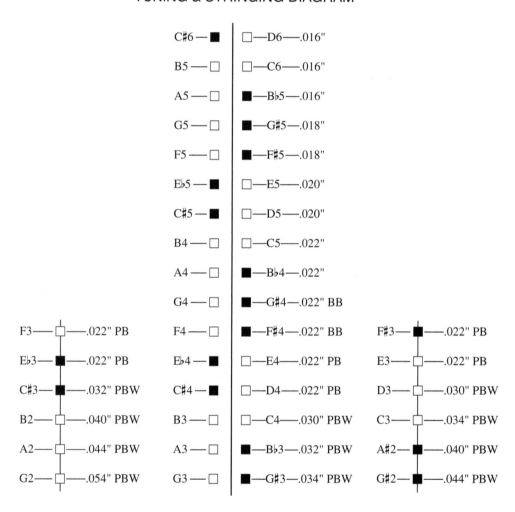

C4 is middle C. □ and ■ indicate white and black bridge markers.
PB indicates phosphor bronze. BB indicates bright bronze.
PBW indicates phosphor bronze wound.
All other strings are plain steel.

Courtesy of Dusty Strings Company (Seattle, WA, USA)

PIANO DULCIMER - Model PD30

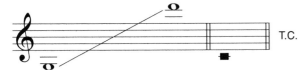

T.C.

This instrument has a single bridge arranged in the piano dulcimer format. Fully chromatic for its 2 1/2 octave range, the bridge cap markers mimic the pattern of white and black notes on the piano.

TUNING & STRINGING DIAGRAM

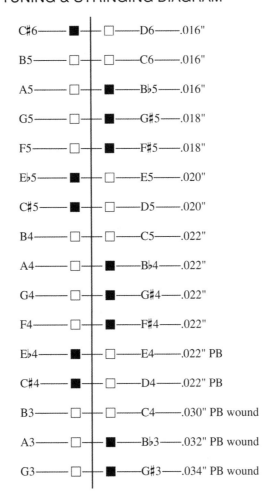

C♯6	■	□	D6 — .016"
B5	□	□	C6 — .016"
A5	□	■	B♭5 — .016"
G5	□	■	G♯5 — .018"
F5	□	■	F♯5 — .018"
E♭5	■	□	E5 — .020"
C♯5	■	□	D5 — .020"
B4	□	□	C5 — .022"
A4	□	■	B♭4 — .022"
G4	□	■	G♯4 — .022"
F4	□	■	F♯4 — .022"
E♭4	■	□	E4 — .022" PB
C♯4	■	□	D4 — .022" PB
B3	□	□	C4 — .030" PB wound
A3	□	■	B♭3 — .032" PB wound
G3	□	■	G♯3 — .034" PB wound

C4 is middle C. □ and ■ indicate white and black bridge markers.
PB indicates phosphor bronze. All other strings are plain steel.

Courtesy of Dusty Strings Company (Seattle, WA, USA)

Traditional or Fifth-Interval Tuning

This tuning scheme is called "fifth-interval" because the treble bridge is a perfect fifth interval above the note on the right. Similarly, each note on the right side of the treble bridge is a fifth interval higher than the adjacent note below it on the bass bridge.

The instrument is tuned in major scale sequences. The scales available with traditional fifth interval tunings are D, G, C, F, A and sometimes E.

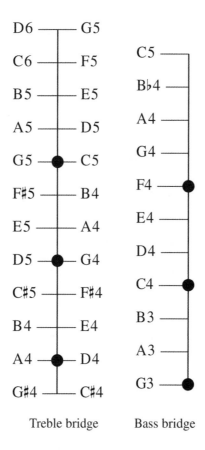

Traditional fifth-interval
tuning scheme

Courtesy of Dusty Strings Company (Seattle, WA, USA)

63

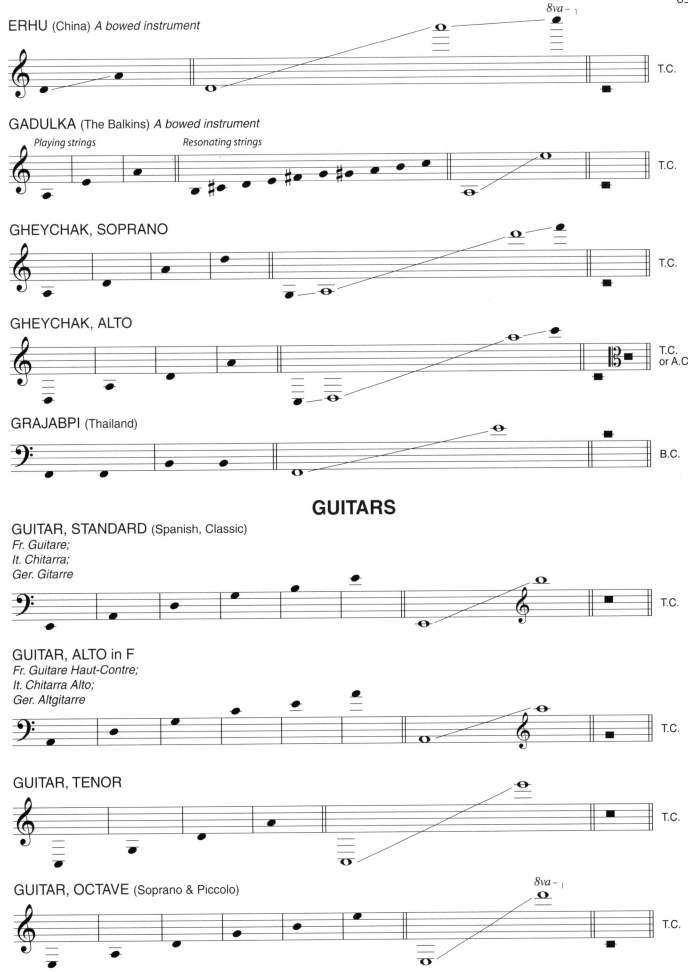

GUITARS

GUITAR, BARITONE

(or)

GUITAR Special Electric with coupling device for extended range

GUITAR, STEEL (Hawaiian)

(or)

GUITAR, BASS & ELECTRIC BASS, 4 STRING (USA)

GUITAR, BASS & ELECTRIC BASS, 5 STRING (USA)

GUITAR, BASS & ELECTRIC BASS, 6 STRING (USA)
Fretted & Fretless

GUITAR, BASS & ELECTRIC BASS, 8 STRING (USA)
Fr. Guitare Basse Electrique;
It. Chitarra Basso Electrico;
Ger. Elektrische Bassgitarre

GUITAR, 12 STRING (Brazil, USA)

GUITARLELE (Japan)

GUITARRA ARGENTINO (Argentina)

GUITARRA de GOLPE (Mexico)

GUITARRA PORTUGESA, Lisboa Variant (Portugal)

GUITARRA PORTUGESA, Coimbra Variant (Portugal)

GUITARRÓN CHILENO (Chile)

GUITARRÓN (Mexican Bass Guitar)

GUQUIN (China)

HALSZITHER, KRIENSER (Switzerland)

HARDINGFELE, Standard Tuning, Hardanger Violin (Norway)

Sympathetic strings

or

This instrument has numerous tunings and is sometimes tuned as a B♭ instrument.

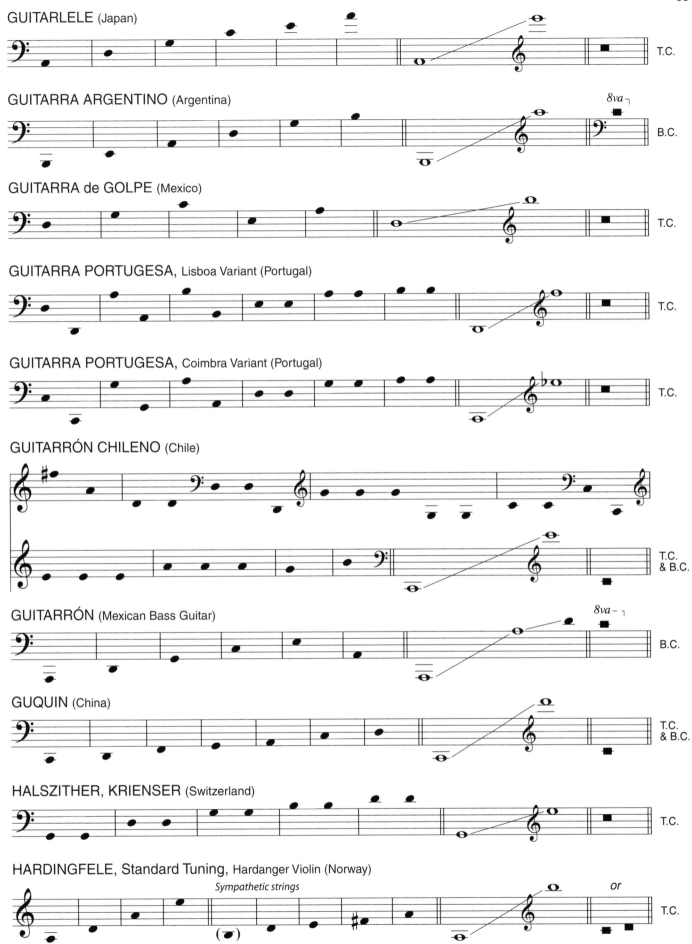

HARPS

CELTIC HARP (36 STRINGS)

Fr. Harpe;
It. Arpa;
Ger. Harfe

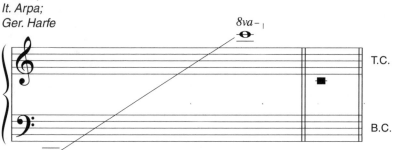

IRISH HARP

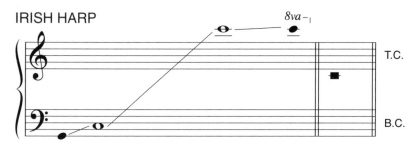

A diatonic instrument. It can be tuned to any key, but <u>no accidentals</u> can be added.

IRISH HARP

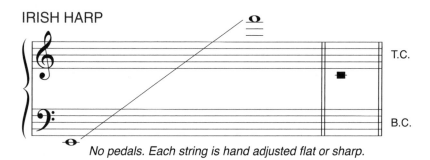

No pedals. Each string is hand adjusted flat or sharp.

MEXICAN HARP

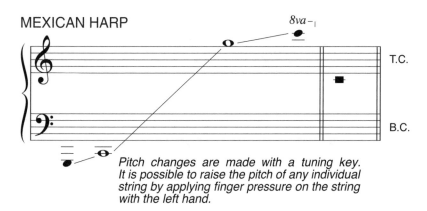

Pitch changes are made with a tuning key. It is possible to raise the pitch of any individual string by applying finger pressure on the string with the left hand.

TROUBADOUR HARP

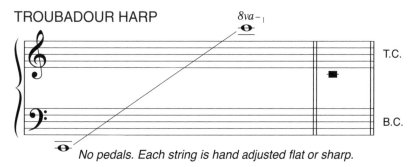

No pedals. Each string is hand adjusted flat or sharp.

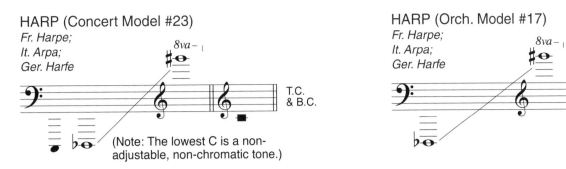

HARP (Concert Model #23)
Fr. Harpe;
It. Arpa;
Ger. Harfe

(Note: The lowest C is a non-adjustable, non-chromatic tone.)

HARP (Orch. Model #17)
Fr. Harpe;
It. Arpa;
Ger. Harfe

THE PEDAL-DIAGRAM

The vertical lines indicate the positions of the seven transposing pedals which have two notch positions from the neutral position of the key of C♭. The depression of any one pedal into the first notch raises all the strings of its name by one semitone. The depression into the second notch raises them another semitone.

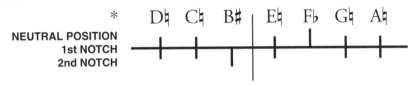

MAJOR CHORD GLISSANDOS

DOMINANT 7th GLISSANDOS

AUGMENTED GLISSANDOS

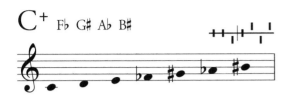

DIMINISHED 7th GLISSANDOS

C#dim C# Db Fb A#

Ddim Db E# G# Bb

D#dim D# Eb Gb B#

Edim Eb Fb A# C#

E#dim E# Fb Ab Cb

F#dim F# Gb B# D#

Gdim Gb A# C# Eb

G#dim G# Ab Cb E#

Adim Ab B# D# F#

A#dim A# Bb Db Fb

Bdim Bb Cb E# G#

B#dim B# Cb Eb Gb

WHOLE TONE SCALES

F♯ G♯ A♯ B♯

C♭ D♭ E♭

PENTATONIC SCALE

F♭ B♯

72

HURDY GURDY or ORGANISTRUM

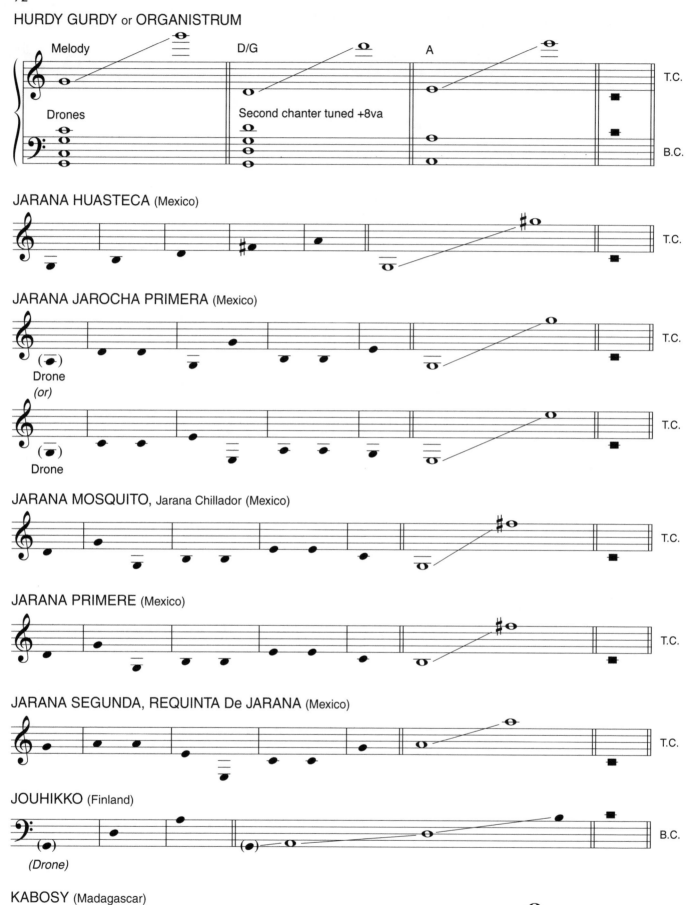

73

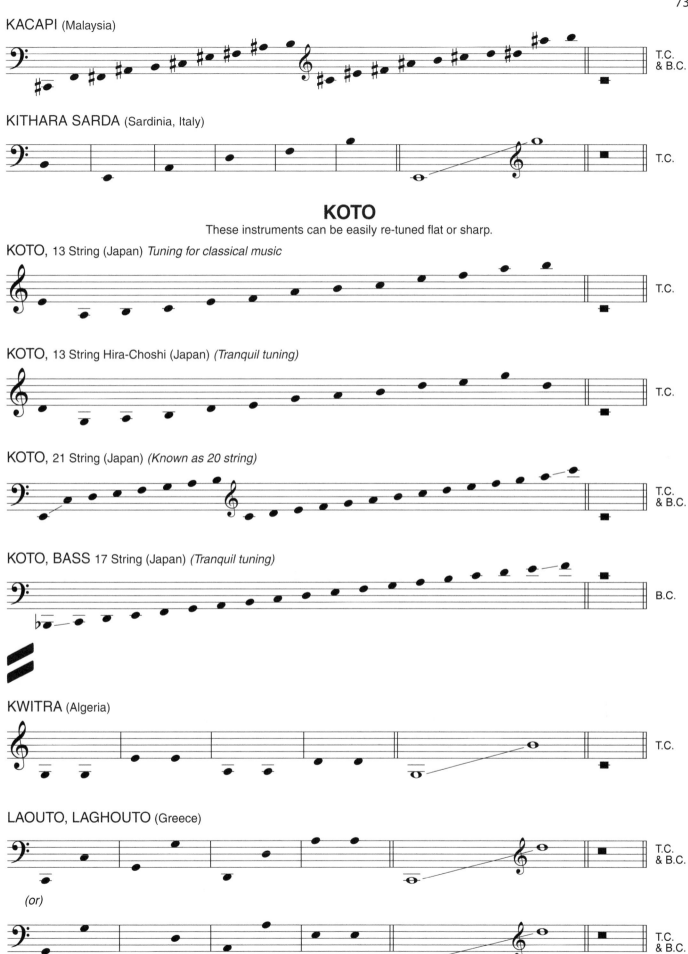

KACAPI (Malaysia) — T.C. & B.C.

KITHARA SARDA (Sardinia, Italy) — T.C.

KOTO
These instruments can be easily re-tuned flat or sharp.

KOTO, 13 String (Japan) *Tuning for classical music* — T.C.

KOTO, 13 String Hira-Choshi (Japan) *(Tranquil tuning)* — T.C.

KOTO, 21 String (Japan) *(Known as 20 string)* — T.C. & B.C.

KOTO, BASS 17 String (Japan) *(Tranquil tuning)* — B.C.

KWITRA (Algeria) — T.C.

LAOUTO, LAGHOUTO (Greece) — T.C. & B.C.

(or) — T.C. & B.C.

LATFIOL, Swedish Violin (Sweden) *(or)*

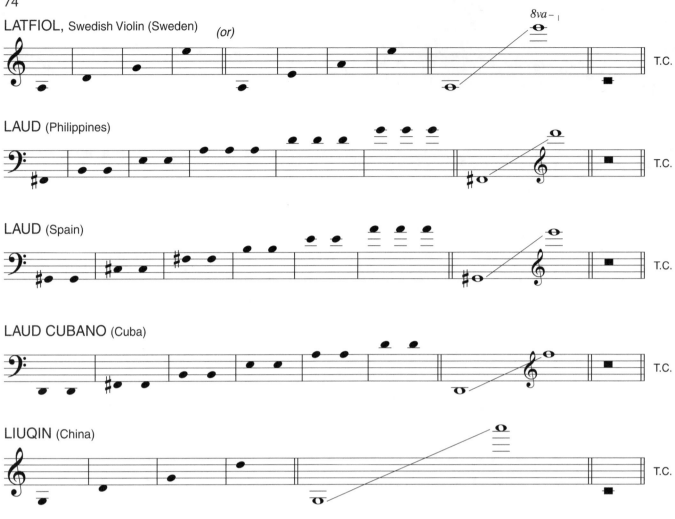

T.C.

LAUD (Philippines)

T.C.

LAUD (Spain)

T.C.

LAUD CUBANO (Cuba)

T.C.

LIUQIN (China)

T.C.

LUTES

Fr. Luth; It: Liuto or Leuto; Ger: Laute

The strings of the Lutes are arranged in courses, of which there are 6 basic courses. Almost all modern Lutes are of the "Renaissance" type and they are written for in both "Tablature" and staff notation.

RENAISSANCE LUTES

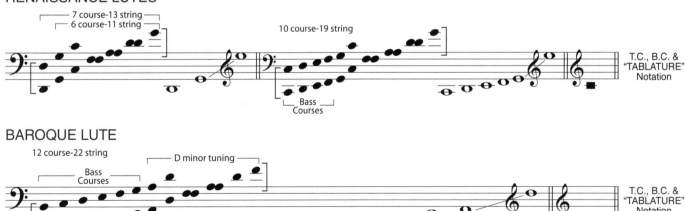

7 course-13 string
6 course-11 string
10 course-19 string
Bass Courses

T.C., B.C. & "TABLATURE" Notation

BAROQUE LUTE

12 course-22 string
Bass Courses
D minor tuning

T.C., B.C. & "TABLATURE" Notation

The full Baroque Lute always has at least 12 courses and 22 strings. They are comprised of the basic 6 courses tuned to the D minor or "Baroque Tuning" (known as the "Nouveau Ton") and 6 or more diatonically tuned bass courses.

LUTE, MEDIEVAL 12 String (Europe)

approximate

T.C., B.C. & "TABLATURE" Notation

LUTE, MEDIEVAL 15 String (Europe)

approximate

8vb –   *8vb –*

T.C., B.C. & "TABLATURE" Notation

LUTE, MEDIEVAL 19 String (Europe)

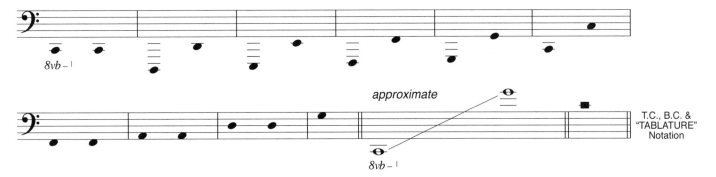

8vb –

approximate

8vb –

T.C., B.C. & "TABLATURE" Notation

LUTAR or GITUTE *Sometimes known as the 6 String Lute*

T.C.

LUTE, CRETAN (Greece) *A bowed instrument*

Common Lyra   Lyraki   Contemporary model

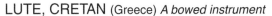

(Drone)

T.C.

MANDOLINS
(USA, Canada, Italy)

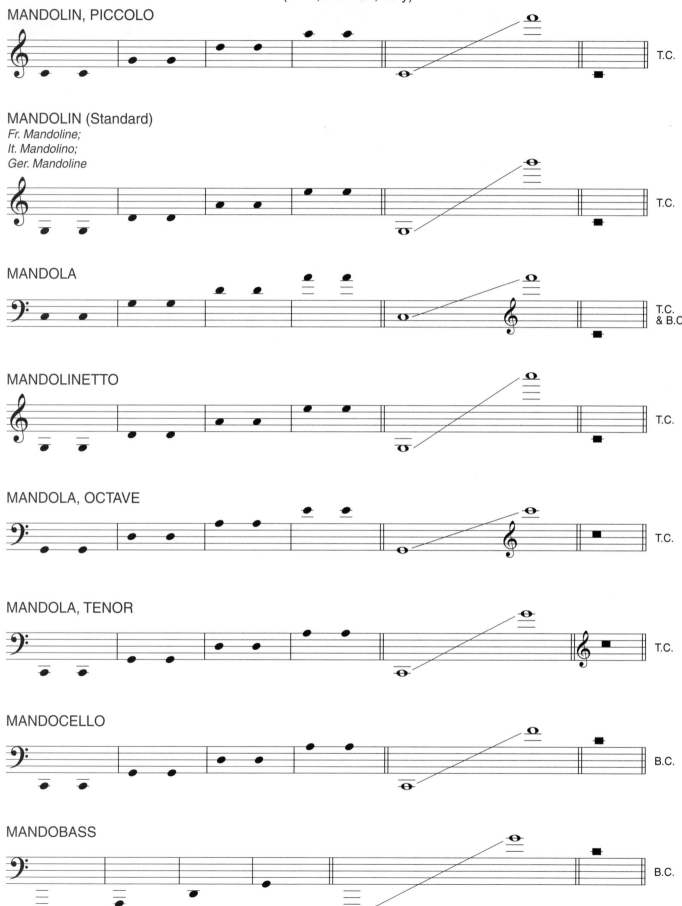

MANDOLIN, PICCOLO

T.C.

MANDOLIN (Standard)
Fr. Mandoline;
It. Mandolino;
Ger. Mandoline

T.C.

MANDOLA

T.C.
& B.C.

MANDOLINETTO

T.C.

MANDOLA, OCTAVE

T.C.

MANDOLA, TENOR

T.C.

MANDOCELLO

B.C.

MANDOBASS

B.C.

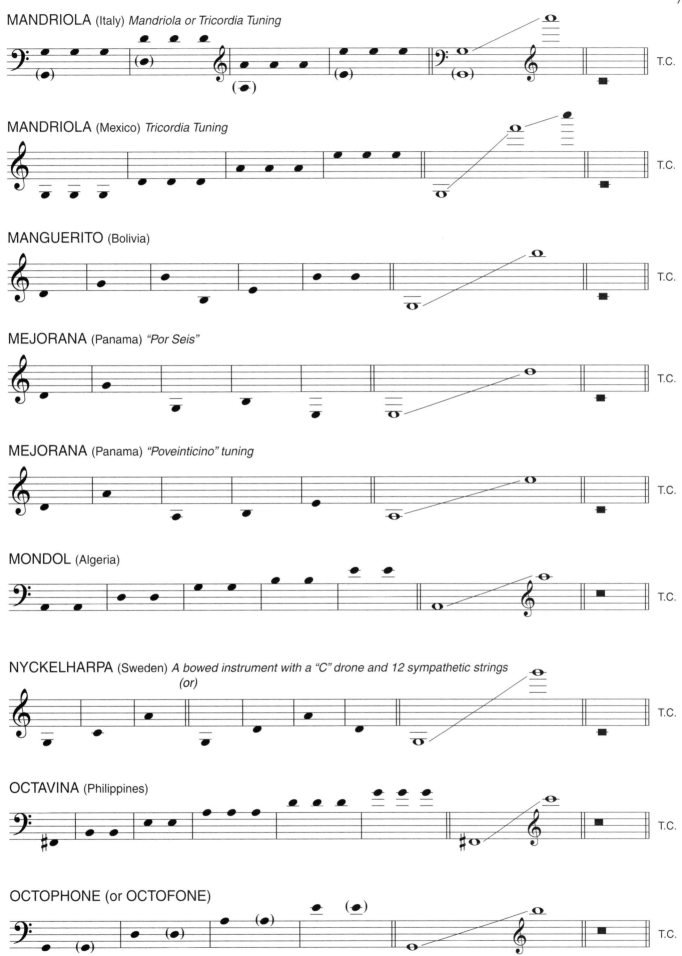

MANDRIOLA (Italy) *Mandriola or Tricordia Tuning*

T.C.

MANDRIOLA (Mexico) *Tricordia Tuning*

T.C.

MANGUERITO (Bolivia)

T.C.

MEJORANA (Panama) *"Por Seis"*

T.C.

MEJORANA (Panama) *"Poveinticino" tuning*

T.C.

MONDOL (Algeria)

T.C.

NYCKELHARPA (Sweden) *A bowed instrument with a "C" drone and 12 sympathetic strings*
(or)

T.C.

OCTAVINA (Philippines)

T.C.

OCTOPHONE (or OCTOFONE)

T.C.

78

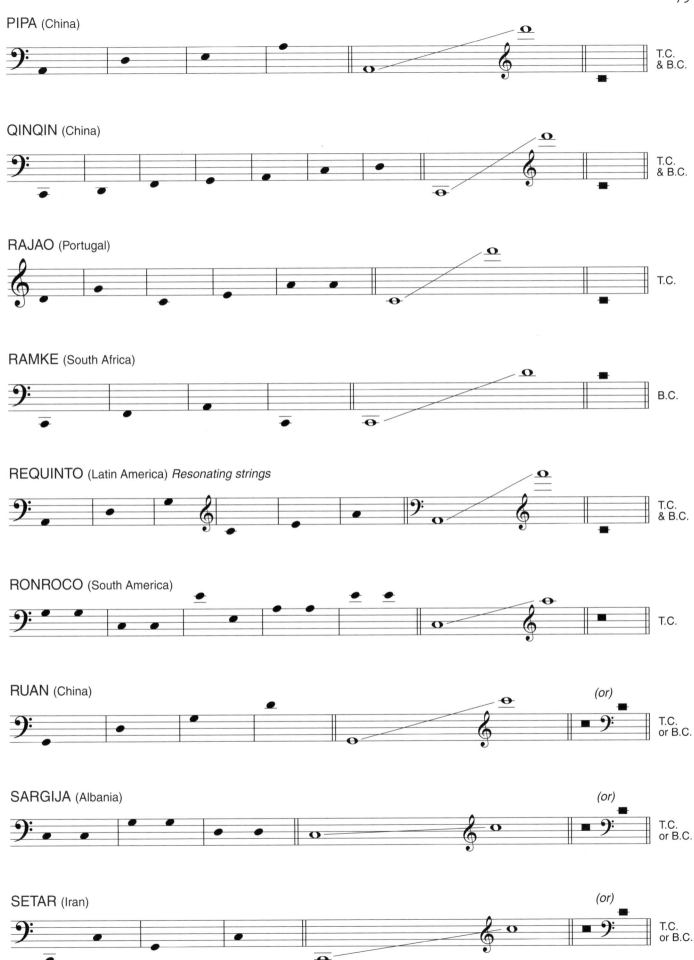

80

SHAMISEN (Japan) *This instrument is usually tuned to the key of the singer*

"Honchoshi" tuning *"Ni Agari" tuning* *"San Sagari" tuning*

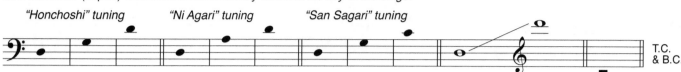

T.C.
& B.C.

SITAR – C♯ (India)

Sympathetic Strings

T.C.
& B.C.

SOCAVON (Columbia, Panama)

(or)

T.C.
& B.C.

*THE STICK® (USA)
FRETBOARD TAPPING INSTRUMENT IN "CLASSIC" TUNING – 10 STRING OPEN TUNING

Melody Bass

T.C.
& B.C.

THE STICK IN "BARITONE MELODY" TUNING – 10 STRING OPEN TUNING

Melody Bass

T.C.
& B.C.

THE GRAND STICK

Melody Bass

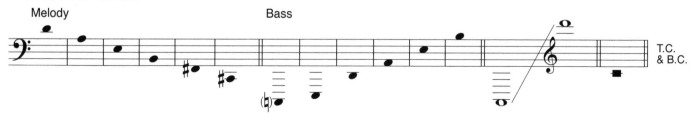

T.C.
& B.C.

* "Stick" and "Chapman Stick" are Federally registered trademarks of Stick Enterprises, Inc. and are used with permission.

STRUMSTICK, G STANDARD (USA) *Primary key is G. Useable keys are C through A.*

T.C.

TAMBURA (Bulgaria)

T.C.

TAMBURA (Macedonia)

T.C.

TAMBURA SAMICA DANGUBICA (Croatia, Serbia)

(or)

T.C.

TAMBURITZAS
(Croatia, Serbia)

G PRIM or BISERNICA – Solo Folk Instrument

8va

T.C.

E PRIM

8va

T.C.

D PRIM

8va

T.C.

A BASPRIM or BRAC

T.C.

continued

(TAMBURITZA)

G BASPRIM Solo Folk Instrument

T.C.

G KONTRA

T.C.

E KONTRA or BUGARIJA — Rhythm Folk Instrument

T.C.

D KONTRA

T.C.

TAMBURITZA CELLO

B.C.

TAR (Iran) *Plus 2 pairs of sympathetic strings tuned at the discretion of the player*

T.C.
& B.C.

TEMBOR (China)

T.C.
& B.C.

TERZIN KITARRA (Malta) *"Sol Guitar" Prim (Lead)*

T.C.
& B.C.

TIPLES

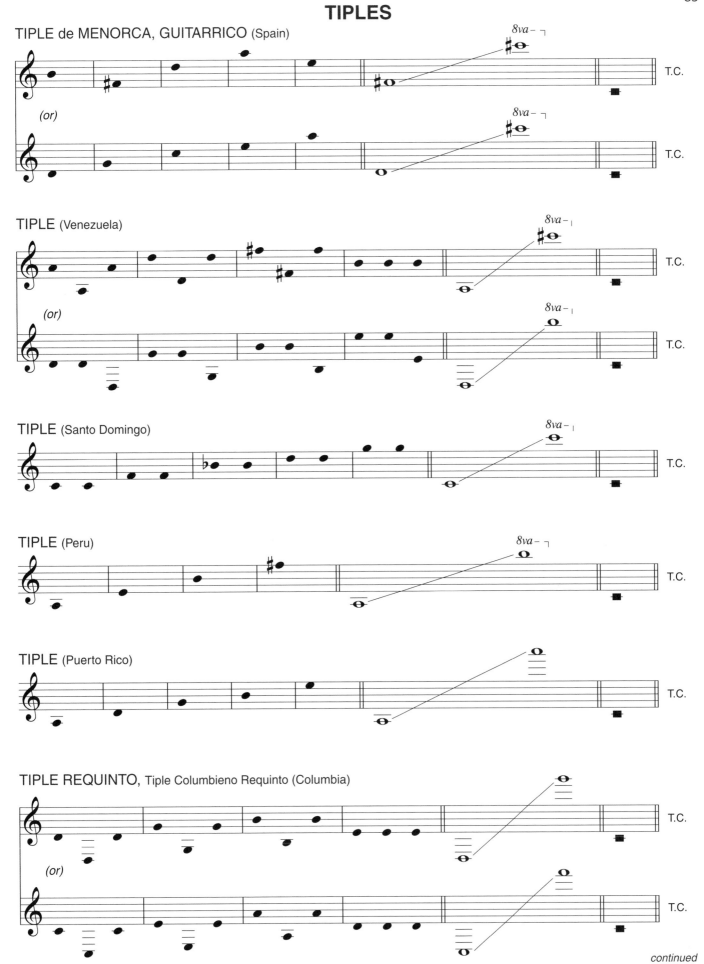

continued

84

TIPLE (Martin, USA)

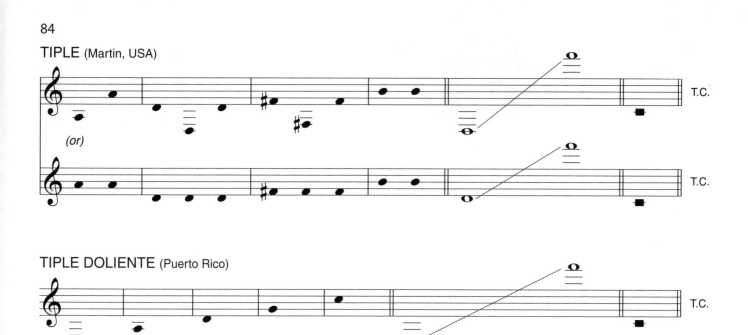

(or)

TIPLE DOLIENTE (Puerto Rico)

T.C.

TIPLE (Argentina)

T.C.

TIPLE COLUMBIANO (Columbia)

T.C.

TIPLE (Canary Islands)

T.C.

TIPLE COLUMBIANO (Columbia, Chile)

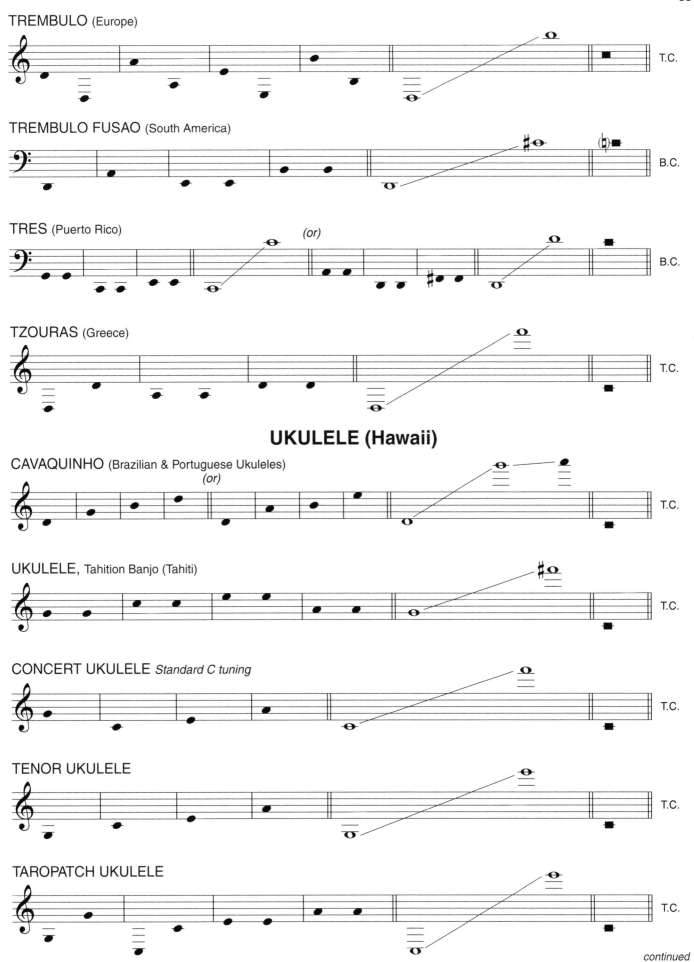

continued

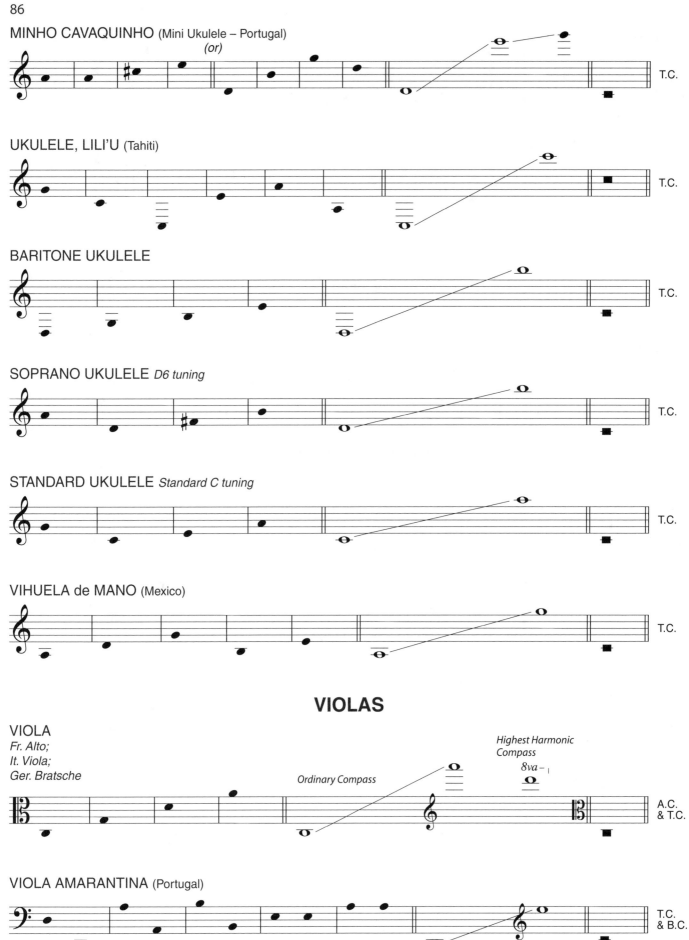

MINHO CAVAQUINHO (Mini Ukulele – Portugal)

(or)

T.C.

UKULELE, LILI'U (Tahiti)

T.C.

BARITONE UKULELE

T.C.

SOPRANO UKULELE *D6 tuning*

T.C.

STANDARD UKULELE *Standard C tuning*

T.C.

VIHUELA de MANO (Mexico)

T.C.

VIOLAS

VIOLA
Fr. Alto;
It. Viola;
Ger. Bratsche

Highest Harmonic
Compass
8va –

Ordinary Compass

A.C.
& T.C.

VIOLA AMARANTINA (Portugal)

T.C.
& B.C.

continued

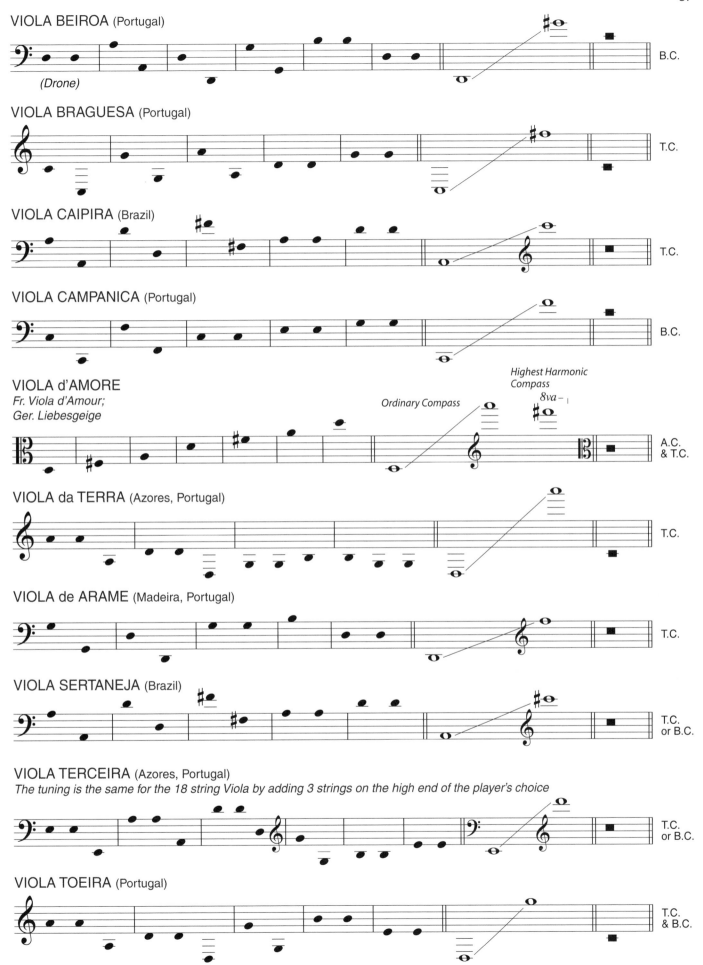

VIOLA BEIROA (Portugal)

(Drone)

B.C.

VIOLA BRAGUESA (Portugal)

T.C.

VIOLA CAIPIRA (Brazil)

T.C.

VIOLA CAMPANICA (Portugal)

B.C.

VIOLA d'AMORE
*Fr. Viola d'Amour;
Ger. Liebesgeige*

Ordinary Compass

Highest Harmonic
Compass
8va –

A.C.
& T.C.

VIOLA da TERRA (Azores, Portugal)

T.C.

VIOLA de ARAME (Madeira, Portugal)

T.C.

VIOLA SERTANEJA (Brazil)

T.C.
or B.C.

VIOLA TERCEIRA (Azores, Portugal)
The tuning is the same for the 18 string Viola by adding 3 strings on the high end of the player's choice

T.C.
or B.C.

VIOLA TOEIRA (Portugal)

T.C.
& B.C.

VIOLIN
Fr. Violon;
It. Violino;
Ger. Violine or Geige

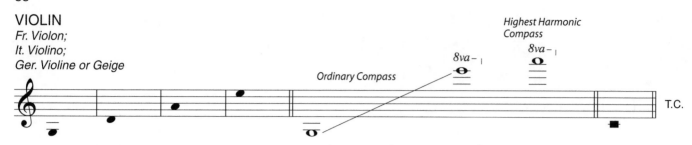

VIOLS

Fr. Viole; It. Viola; Ger. Gambe, Kniegeige or Viole

A family of bowed string instruments which were widely used in the 16th and 17th century and have been revived for the performance of music of that period.

DESCANT or TREBLE–VIOL

TENOR–VIOL or VIOLA da BRACCIO

BASS–VIOL or VIOLA da GAMBA

WALAYCHO, Hualaycho, Maulincho (South America) *F6 tuning*

WALAYCHO, Hualaycho, Maulincho (South America) *G6 tuning*

WALDZITHER (Germany)

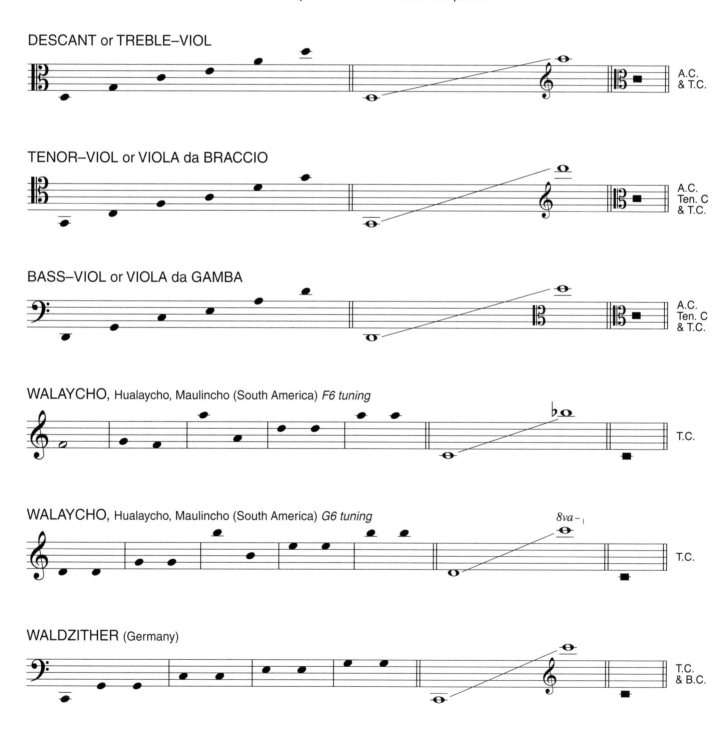

YUEQUIN (China)

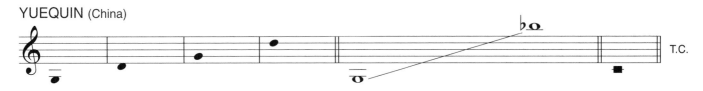

T.C.

YUEQUIN (Taiwan)

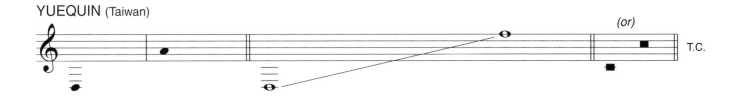

(or)

T.C.

ZITHERS

ZITHER (Treble & Consort)
Fr. Zither;
It. Zittera;
Ger. Schlagzither, Primzither
(Treble Zither) (Concert Zither)

Melody Strings

T.C.
& B.C.

Accompaniment Strings
As Written – Sounds 8va basso

*Alternate tuning

ALTO ZITHER (Treble & Concert)
Fr. Zither Alto;
It. Zittera Alto;
Ger. Elegie, Alt or Liederzither

Melody Strings

T.C.
& B.C.

Accompaniment Strings
As Written – Sounds 8va basso

*Alternate tuning

BAROQUE & RENAISSANCE INSTRUMENTS

KRUMHORNS (Renaissance Oboes)

SOPRANO

T.C.

TENOR
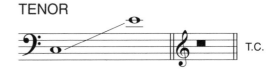
T.C.

ALTO (in F)
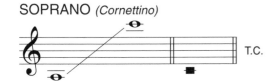
T.C.

BASS (in F)

B.C.

CORNETTOS (ZINKES)

SOPRANO *(Cornettino)*

T.C.

TENOR

A.C.
& B.C.

SOPRANO (in A)
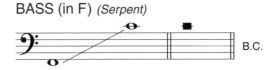
T.C.

BASS (in F) *(Serpent)*
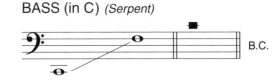
B.C.

ALTO (in F)
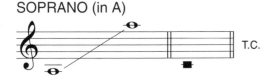
T.C.

BASS (in C) *(Serpent)*
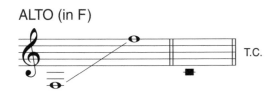
B.C.

SACKBUTS

ALTO (in E♭)
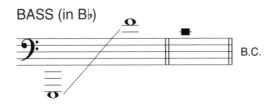
A.C.
& T.C.

TENOR (in B♭)

B.C.
& Ten.C.

BASS (in B♭)

B.C.

TURKISH SHAWM (Turkey) *A primitive Oboe*

T.C.

SUPPLEMENTARY INSTRUMENTS

AUTOHARP (12 Chord)

T.C.
& B.C.

CHORD BARS

Gm B♭ A⁷ C⁷ Dm F E⁷ G⁷ Am C D⁷ G

THEREMIN

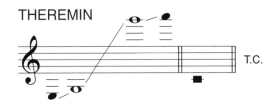

T.C.

MUSETTE (2-Pipe Bagpipe)

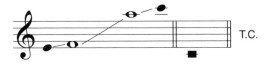

T.C.

HIGHLAND BAGPIPE

CHANTER

(sounds approx. 1/4 tone sharp)

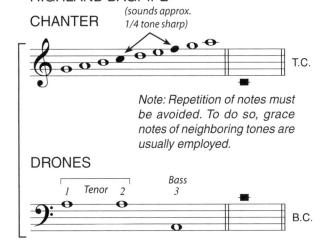

T.C.

Note: Repetition of notes must be avoided. To do so, grace notes of neighboring tones are usually employed.

HANDBELLS

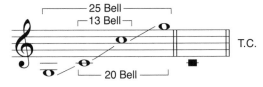

T.C.

DRONES

B.C.

VOICES
OPERATIC

COLORATURA SOPRANO
Fr. Dessus Coloratura;
It. Soprano Coloratura;
Ger. Koloratursopran

T.C.

LYRIC SOPRANO
Fr. Dessus Légère;
It. Soprano di Grazia, Soprano Leggiero;
Ger. Lyrischer Sopran

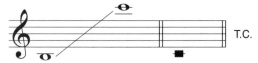

T.C.

DRAMATIC SOPRANO
Fr. Dessus Dramatique;
It. Soprano Drammatico, Robusto di Forza;
Ger. Heldensopran

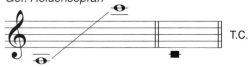

T.C.

MEZZO SOPRANO
Fr. Bas-Dessus;
It. Mezzo Soprano;
Ger. Halbsopran

T.C.

CONTRALTO
Fr. Contralto;
It. Contralto;
Ger. Kontraalt

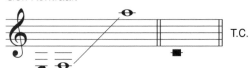

T.C.

LYRIC TENOR
Fr. Ténor Légère;
It. Tenor di Grazia, Tenor Leggiero;
Ger. Lyrischer Tenor

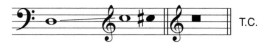

T.C.

DRAMATIC TENOR
Fr. Ténor Dramatique;
It. Tenor Drammatico, Robusto, di Forza;
Ger. Heldentenor

T.C.

BARITONE
Fr. Barytone;
It. Baritono;
Ger. Bariton

B.C.

BASS BARITONE
Fr. Barytone Basse, Basse-Taille;
It. Baritono Basso;
Ger. Bass Bariton

B.C.

BASS
Fr. Basse;
It. Basso;
Ger. Bass

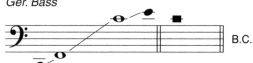

B.C.

93

ADULT MIXED CHORUS
(Professional Groups)

1st SOPRANO

T.C.

2nd SOPRANO

T.C.

1st ALTO

T.C.

2nd ALTO

T.C.

1st TENOR

T.C.

2nd TENOR

T.C.

BARITONE

B.C.

BASS

B.C.

HIGH SCHOOL MIXED CHORUS

1st SOPRANO

T.C.

1st TENOR

T.C.

2nd SOPRANO

T.C.

2nd TENOR

T.C.

1st ALTO

T.C.

1st BASS

B.C.

2nd ALTO

T.C.

2nd BASS

B.C.

BOYS CHOIR
(Trained Boy-Sopranos)

1st SOPRANO

T.C.

2nd SOPRANO

T.C.

ALTO

T.C.

CHILDREN
(Boys & Girls – Untrained)

T.C.

INDEX

100

FRENCH

Accordeon – 27
Alto – 86
Baryton – 17, 19, 92
Baryton Basse (Basse-Taille) – 92
Basse – 92
Basse a Pistons – 19
Bas-Dessus – 92
Basson – 7
Bombardon – 17
Bugle – 16
Bugle Alto – 15
Bugle Dessus – 15
Bugle Haute-Contre – 15
Bugle Ténor, Barytone – 19
Carillon (Jeu de Timbre) – 23–24
Clarinette – 6, 9–10
Clavecin – 28
Clavicorde – 28
Cloches – 23
Contralto – 92
Contre Basse – 52
Contrebasson – 7
Cor Anglais – 7
Cor-a-pistons – 12
Cor de Basset – 10
Cor de Chasse – 12
Cornet – 15
Dessus Coloratura – 92
Dessus Dramatique – 92
Dessus Légère – 92
Fifre – 6
Flûte – 6
Flûte à Bec – 22
Guitare – 63
Guitare Haut-Contre – 63
Guitare Basse Electrique – 64
Harpe – 66–71
Hautbois – 7
Jeu de Timbre (Carillon) – 23–24, 46
Luth – 74–75
Mandoline – 76
Marimba Basse – 24
Musette Accordeon – 27
Orgue – 30–44
Petite Flute – 6
Petite Saxhorn, Petite Bugle á Pistons – 17
Petite Tuba en Ut – 19
Piano, Pianoforte – 27
Sarrusophone – 8
Saxophone – 11
Ténor Dramatique – 92

Ténor Légère – 92
Timbales – 25–26
Trombone – 18
Trompette – 13–14
Tuba Basse – 17
Viola d'Amour – 87
Violon – 88
Violoncelle – 54
Xylophon (Claquebois) – 26
Zither – 89
Zither Alto – 89

ITALIAN

Accordeon – 27
Arpa – 66–71
Arpicordo (Clavicembalo) – 28
Baritono – 92
Baritono Basso – 92
Basso – 92
Campane (Campanelle) – 23
Campanetta – 23–24
Chitarra – 63
Chitarra Alto – 63
Chitarra Basso Electrico – 64
Clarinetto – 6, 9–10
Clarino Contrabasso – 10
Clarone – 10
Clavicembalo (Arpicordo) – 28
Clavicordo – 28
Contrabasso – 52
Contrafagotto – 7
Contralto – 92
Cornetto (Cornettino) – 15, 90
Corno di Bassetto – 10
Corno Inglese – 7
Corno Ventile – 12
Eufonio – 19
Fagotto – 7
Flauto – 6
Flauto Dolce – 22
Flautone – 6
Flauto Basso – 6
Flauto Soprano – 6
Flicorno – 15
Flicorno Soprano – 15
Flicorno Alto – 15
Flicorno Tenore – 19
Liuto or Leuto – 74–75
Mandolino – 76
Marimba Basso – 24
Mezzo Soprano – 92

GERMAN

Robert G. (Bob) Bornstein
Violinist, Arranger, Orchestrator and Copyist

Robert Bornstein began his career as the youngest violinist in the New Jersey Youth Orchestra. While still in his teens, he taught himself to transpose and copy the orchestra parts for the songs "Angelina" and "Don't Squeeza da Banana" for the Louis Prima Orchestra. He began to study arranging and orchestrating for several traveling orchestras in New Jersey.

On the day after high school graduation, Bob boarded a train for Los Angeles, CA. Upon arrival, he transferred his professional membership to the LA Musicians Union, Local 47. After a few months of side-lining motion pictures, parties and other casual work, he joined an orchestra that was hired by the Last Frontier Hotel in Las Vegas. During this time, he traveled to Los Angeles one night a week (after playing at the Frontier until midnight) to take lessons in orchestration and composition from classical film composer Ernst Toch. He then returned to Nevada the same day for the evening performance.

After this engagement, Bob returned to LA as a freelance musician. In 1947 he was introduced to Jimmy Durante by his piano player, who had written a new composition for which Bob had made a full orchestral arrangement and had recorded. Jimmy was so impressed that he made Bob the chief arranger of all of his performances – live, television, and for his publishing company. Bob had a great relationship with Jimmy and spent many mornings having breakfast with him at Jimmy's home in Beverly Hills. When Bob received a draft notice at the beginning of the Korean War (1951), Jimmy sent a letter to the draft board requesting that he be excused. Of course, the request for release from military service was refused and Bob was inducted into the U.S. Army. Bob and Jimmy were very close friends until Jimmy's passing in 1980.

After Bob's induction into the army, he was released from basic training and sent to the U.S. Military Academy at West Point, where he served four years as Chief Arranger to the USMA Band (comprised of 100 musicians). He received a special commendation from commanding officer Lt. Col. Francis E. Resta.

After completing his military service in 1954, Bob returned to Los Angeles and freelanced, spending most of his time at major motion picture studios. In 1972 he was selected to supervise music preparation for all of Lorimar Television's programs, a position he held until Lorimar's closing in 1993. Bob worked at most of the other studios at different periods of time – the last being Paramount Pictures, where he was in charge of music production for over thirty years. During this time he produced and prepared the music for the Academy Awards (32 years) and the Peoples Choice Awards, as well as numerous motion pictures such as "Avatar" and "Titanic" by James Horner, with whom he worked for many years. Bob is also grateful to his dear friend, composer, pianist and conductor Bill Conti, for the opportunity to work with him on more Academy Awards shows than anyone else at that time, as well as numerous films and concerts.

Here is a list of just some of the composers that Bob has worked with over the years. He also has worked on over 600 films in addition to the many TV shows and series.

Addisson, John	Howard, James Newton	Previn, André
Amfitheatrof, Daniele	Isham, Mark	Raksin, David
Armstrong, Craig	Jarre, Maurice	Riddle, Nelson
Arnold, David	Jones, Quincy	Rosenman, Leonard
Barry, John	Kaper, Bronisław	Rosenthal, Laurence
Bennett, Robert Russell	Korngold, Erich Wolfgang	Rota, Nino
Bernstein, Elmer	Lai, Francis	Rózsa, Miklós
Conti, Bill	Legrand, Michel	Rubenstein, Arthur
Delerue, Georges	Lilley, Joseph	Scharf, Walter
Dolan, Robert Emmett	Mancini, Henry	Schifrin, Lalo
Deutsch, Adolph	Menken, Alan	Shaiman, Marc
Doyle, Patrick	Mockridge, Cyril	Shire, David
Elfman, Danny	Morricone, Ennio	Shore, Howard
Fenton, George	Morris, John	Silvestri, Alan
Friedhofer, Hugo	Murray, Lyn	Steiner, Max
Goldsmith, Jerry	Newman, Alfred	Tiomkin, Dimitri
Gold, Ernest	Newman, David	Tunick, Jonathan
Goldenberg, William	Newman, Randy	Waxman, Franz
Goldenthal, Elliot	Newman, Thomas	Williams, Harry-Gregson
Goodman, Miles	North, Alex	Williams, John
Green, John	Ottman, John	Yared, Gabriel
Hamlisch, Marvin	Poledouris, Basil	Young, Christopher
Herrmann, Bernard	Portman, Rachel	Young, Victor
Horner, James	Powell, John	Zimmer, Hans